Wheaton Public Library
225 N. Cross
Wheaton, Illinois 60187
(630) 668-1374

DEMCO

Winning in the Options Market

in the

Options
Market

A STREETWISE

◆

TRADER SHOWS YOU

◆

HOW TO OUTSMART

◆

THE PROS

ALLAN S.
Lyons

PROBUS PUBLISHING COMPANY
Chicago, Illinois
Cambridge, England

ISBN 1-55738-431-2

Printed in the United States of America

BB

1 2 3 4 5 6 7 8 9 0

*To my daughters Wendy and Jody, the finest
dividends a father could hope for.*

Table of Contents

1. Basics

Ideally, investors who read this book, both private and institutional, will have a basic knowledge of options. Those who wish to be sure they haven't overlooked some of the basic aspects will want to quickly review this chapter.

PART I: COMMON MISCONCEPTIONS

In which we learn that unless you are psychic and can call the market consistently, using puts as insurance to protect stocks from a drop in the market is guaranteed to cost you more than it will save you (though the commission business will earn you the deep-felt gratitude of your broker).

Table of Contents

Table of Contents

Table of Contents

Table of Contents

bit more risk, expands both downside protection and upside potential.

This is the second of the two option strategies likely to pay off consistently. Unlike covered call writing and covered portfolio writing, which are low in risk, this is a strategy for investors willing to accept much higher risk to tap the really huge profits options can generate. It is another strategy you won't find in other books. Based on published recommendations, a similar strategy has been profitable, on average, each year since first recommended in 1980. Over this entire span, it has generated indicated compound average annual returns in excess of 70% a year.

In which we discover that if your object is to sell over-priced options, the place to dig for them is in low-priced neighborhoods . . . that if you must select blindfolded (heaven forbid), write low-priced, out-of-the-money calls on low-priced stocks . . . for ever-optimistic, investors overpay for "cheap" options, taking the short odds in the hope of a big payoff . . . and so sellers, who know what they're about and who diversify adequately to spread their risk, in time typically make out like bandits.

PART V: PORTFOLIO MANAGEMENT

It is here that we put it all together—how to construct a portfolio that targets an acceptable level of risk; how to diversify properly in order to put the odds to work for you; and under what conditions positions should be closed out or replaced.

Table of Contents

List of Exhibits

List of Exhibits

List of Exhibits

Basics

Ideally, investors who read this book, both private and institutional, will have a basic knowledge of options. Those who wish to be sure they haven't overlooked some of the basic aspects will want to quickly review this chapter.

IN THIS CHAPTER: ◆ Options, What Are They? ◆ Listed Options ◆ Exercise ◆ Why Buy an Option? ◆ Option Premiums ◆ Option Mathematics ◆ How Option Premiums are Set ◆ "Naked" versus "Covered" Options ◆ Margin ◆ The Option Market Expands ◆ Index Options ◆ Placing an Order ◆ The Bid/Asked Spread and Liquidity ◆ Commissions ◆ Spreads ◆ The Changing Market ◆ Covered Calls ◆ Closing Option Positions

OPTIONS: WHAT ARE THEY?

An option is a contract between two parties—the writer or seller of the option and the buyer. The option contract defines the rights of each party. Stock options come in two kinds: calls and puts. A call gives the option buyer the right to purchase shares:

1. In a specified stock (or stock index);

2. At a specified price (called the exercise or "strike" price); and

3. During a specified period (or on a specific date).

A put gives the option buyer the right to sell a specified stock (or stock index) at a specified price during a specified period (or on a specific date).

For example, you might buy a March 50 call on GM. That would give you the right to buy GM stock at $50 a share at any time before the option expired in March. Or, if you bought a March 50 put on GM, you could sell GM stock at $50 a share at any time before the option expired.

At one time, it was necessary for someone who wanted to buy an option to locate someone willing to sell. This was usually arranged through the broker, but often ads were placed in the financial columns of newspapers such as *The Wall Street Journal*. Option contracts so arranged were for whatever number of shares and at whatever exercise price the two parties agreed to.

Listed Options

Needless to say, this was rather unwieldy. Moreover, buyers and writers of options who later changed their minds found it very cumbersome to close out positions prior to expiration. The Chicago Board Options Exchange (CBOE) streamlined the process in 1973 when they created standardized options. These "listed" options:

◆ Are for 100 shares of stock. (In the event of stock dividends or splits, an existing option may, however, later become an option on a greater number of shares.)

◆ Are opened initially for a period of nine months.

◆ Expire at the close of trading on the third Friday of the designated month.

◆ Exercise at preset prices. With low-priced stocks, the lowest strike will be $5. Above that, strikes rise by $2.50 intervals up to $25 (at $7.50, $10, $12.50, etc.). Strikes above $25 are at $5 intervals (e.g., $30, $35, $40, etc.).

◆ When a given month's options expire, new put and call options are created that expire nine months later. These are struck at about the current price of the stock, the next higher strike, and the next lower strike. For example, after the GM January options expire (on the third Friday of January), if GM

were 41, October options would be created struck at
$35, $40, and $45.

◆ As the price of the stock rises or falls, additional
strikes are created so that for each month of expiration, there is always a strike above and a strike below the price of the stock. If, for example, GM were
to climb to $47 in May, put and call options would
be created that expire in October with a strike price
of $50. In the case of a volatile stock, you may find
10 or more different strikes for a particular month
of expiration.

Because options are contracts between two parties, the
buyer and the seller, an option does not come into existence until both a buyer and a seller are found. The exchange makes this relatively easy. Because listed options are
recorded on the books of the options exchange, the name
of the buyer and the seller of a particular option are not
yoked together. Rather, the exchange simply makes certain
that there are sufficient buyers and sellers to account for
the open contracts for a specific option. (Brokers' names
rather than the individual buyers or sellers are listed in the
exchange's books; it is the brokers' job to keep track of the
buyers and sellers.)

Once an option contract is opened, however, it becomes easy for the original buyer or seller to locate someone through the exchange to take over his position. Thus, a
seller can normally buy back his contract at any time and a
buyer can normally sell off his contract at any time. The
exchange makes certain, however, that there is always a
buyer for every seller. It also keeps track of whether a new
contract was opened or an existing contract closed out.

Exercise

The buyer of a call who wants to acquire the underlying stock may exercise his option at any time up until expiration. If he exercises, he must pay the writer of the option the strike price. For example, if an owner of a call on GM struck at $45 exercised the option, he would pay the writer of the call $4,500 and would receive 100 shares of GM stock. The actual transfer of the stock to his account would be handled by the broker, who would charge him the same commission he would pay if he purchased the stock on the market. The price originally paid for the option is additional.

The holder who exercised a GM put struck at $45 would deliver 100 shares of GM (through his broker) for which he would be paid $4,500. Again, commissions would be charged at the same rate as the stock was sold on the market.

Less than 10% of all options are exercised, however. Rarely do option buyers wish to acquire the stock; options are bought in hopes of selling the options at a whopping profit if the price of the underlying stock shoots up. Indeed, exercise is a disadvantage, for commissions on the exchange of stock are many times greater than for selling the option.

There are two kinds of options in respect to the exercise privilege—American style and European style. American-style options can be exercised at any time during their life; European-style options can be exercised only on the day they expire.

At expiration, the exchange will automatically exercise an open option for an owner who failed to exercise—if exercise would be likely to yield a profit for him after commissions are taken into consideration.

CHAPTER 1

Why Buy an Option?

In a word, LEVERAGE. A small investment in an option can yield an enormous profit on just a small move in the stock. For example, say you paid $0.50 for a GM call struck at 45 when the stock was 43. Two weeks later, the stock rises to $47, a 9% gain. Your call will then be worth at least $2, up 400%.

But when the potential rewards are high, so too is the risk. If, by expiration, GM didn't rise, or even if it rose only as high as 45, your call would expire worthless. You'd lose 100% of your investment.

On average, the typical option has 10 times the profit potential of common stocks, and 10 times the risk. To put this in perspective, if options are fairly priced so that neither the buyer nor the seller has an advantage, if you bought 10 options, you might reap a 10-to-1 profit on one and lose the entire amount you invested in the other nine. Clearly, then, it's necessary to find a way to tilt the odds in your favor. That's what this book is about.

Option Premiums

The fee or price that a buyer pays to the seller of an option is called the premium. Prices are always quoted per share. Thus, an option quoted at $5 would cost $500 (plus commissions).

An option is said to be "at the money," "in the money," or "out of the money" depending on the price of the stock relative to the option strike. A GM October 45 call option would be at the money if the stock was $45, in the money if the stock was above $45, and out of the money if the stock was below $45.

An in-the-money option has a "tangible" or "intrinsic value." A call struck at $45, for example, has a tangible value of $2 a share when the stock is $47; the call enables you to buy stock for $45 that can be resold for $47. If the stock was below $45, the call would have no tangible value. Puts, of course, work the other way: a put struck at $45 has a tangible value if the stock is below $45, for the holder can sell stock at $45 that can be purchased at a lower price.

The option premium, the price a seller demands from the buyer, reflects both the tangible value of the option and its "time value," the time remaining during which the option's value might increase. The time value of the premium also takes into account the volatility of the underlying stock. The more volatile the stock, the greater the chance of a large move in price of the stock before expiration and a huge jump in the value of the option. That translates into greater risk for the seller. (Other factors that influence the option premium are the risk-free interest rate available on alternate investments and the dividend yield of the stock, but these are far less important.)

Option Mathematics

How much math should you know to be comfortable with options? Actually, very little. Once you go beyond the Black-Scholes model, a model used to estimate the value of an option, or other models that claim they do it even better, there is little but simple mathematics to apply. But even the value of these models is brought into question by the experts—for some use one while some use others—a clear indication that no one model is fully in tune with the market.

You should, however, be at home with the concept of probability, the odds that an event will or will not occur. It is not coincidental that option traders who trade for their house are often recruited from bridge players, a game that requires a keen understanding of probability. You may be surprised to learn, in addition, that logic and philosophy are also more important in trading options than all but the simplest mathematics.

> For those who enjoy logic puzzles, try this one. It was posed to a young fellow who worked for me when he applied for a position as an option trader. You are given a pitcher with a large quantity of water, a glass that holds three ounces, and another that holds seven ounces. (Neither of the glasses have calibrations.) How can you measure out exactly five ounces of water? (There are two ways. Good luck. If you don't work out the answer, don't give up on options . . . but don't apply for that job.)

How Option Premiums Are Set

Theoretically, option premiums are set so that neither the option buyer nor the seller has an advantage. A call option that is estimated to be worth $3.75 should sell for $3.75. Of course, sellers will want more and buyers will want to pay less. But if trading volume in that option is large and supply and demand are in balance, the price may well settle at that level.

Since the price of the option is based on the stock's future volatility, which no one knows, both the buyer and the seller must estimate how volatile the stock will be in order to arrive at what they believe is the "right" price.

"Naked" versus "Covered" Options

The purchase or sale of an option is said to be naked if an offsetting position in the same stock is not held in the portfolio. The most common hedged position is a "covered call." It combines the sale of one call against each 100 shares of the underlying stock held long. This position is "covered" because if the call is exercised and the writer is required to deliver stock, he doesn't have to go out and buy it but simply delivers shares he already owns. It is hedged because if the stock drops in value, part or all of the loss will be offset by the premium received for selling the call. On the other hand, if the stock rises beyond a certain point, part of the gain is forfeited to the buyer of the call.

Covered call writing is one of the two most attractive ways an investor can use options. Whereas most option strategies are very high in risk, covered call writing is very low in risk. In fact, a covered call writer is exposed to only about half the risk of common stocks. You would expect, as a result, that your returns would be smaller than you'd be likely to earn holding common stocks, for returns and risk normally go hand-in-hand. Surprisingly, this is not the case. Covered call writing normally yields larger returns!

Option positions can also be hedged with offsetting option positions. For example, if you sold a March 50 GM call, you might hedge that position by buying a March 45 GM call. When you sold the March 50 call, you became at risk if the stock climbed above 50. The March 45 call that you bought, however, fully covers any loss on the other. As long as the long call (the call purchased) has a lower strike and expires no earlier than the short call, the position is fully covered.

Any other purchase or sale of an option is considered "naked" or uncovered.

Margin

Options must be bought or sold in a margin account. Before an account may be opened, it is the broker's responsibility to determine whether options are appropriate to your financial situation. When you buy an option, the full price must be paid by the settlement date, normally one business day from date of purchase. If securities are held in the account that are marginable, you may borrow against them to cover the cost.

The buyer of an option can never lose more than the original cost, so he has no further liability. The seller of an option, however, may be liable for many times the original price of the option if the stock moves against him. For example, if you sold a March 45 GM call priced at $1 and at expiration the stock was at $50, it would cost you $5 to buy it back, five times the amount you received for it. Sellers, then, must put up as security more than the price of the option. Typically, a seller's outlay is three times the price of the option. Thus, if you sold a call for $1, you'd have to put up about $3. Margin requirements are recalculated daily, however. If the stock moves against you, additional margin will be required.

Margin requirements for writing equity options and narrow-based index options are equal to 20% of the price of the underlying stock (or index) less the amount the option is out of the money, with a minimum of 10% of the price of the underlying stock. The option premium is added to that. Thus, if GM was 45, the margin on a March 50 GM call selling for $2 would be as shown on the next page.

20% × stock price ($45) =	$9
Less the amount out of the money ($50 – $45)	–5
Option Premium	+2
Margin (per share)	$6
Minimum margin calculation:	
10% × stock price ($45) =	$4.50
Option Premium	2.00
Minimum margin (per share)	$6.50

Since the minimum margin requirement is higher, margin would be $6.50 a share. Note, however, that the option premium received on the sale of the call can be applied against the margin requirement, so the net out-of-pocket amount the writer would have to post is $4.50.

Margin on broad-based index options is equal to 15% of the price of the underlying index plus the option premium. Again, this may be reduced by the amount the option is out of the money, but minimum margin here, again, is 10% of the value of the index plus the option premium.

Note, however, that securities may be posted for margin (at their marginable value) in lieu of cash. In any event, it is rarely wise to put up cash for margin purposes unless your broker will credit interest on the cash to your account. Otherwise, it is usually advantageous to post T-bills, which are 90% marginable. In this way, rather than standing idle, the funds posted for margin earn interest.

The Options Market Expands

Listed call options began trading in 1973 and soon became popular with investors. At first available only on a handful of stocks, by the end of 1970 the number mounted to 200 and continued to expand, topping 500 by the end of 1990.

Trading in puts began in 1977 but never became quite as popular. A better measure of the explosive growth can be seen in the number of option series. (A March 45 GM call would be one "series," a March 50 GM call would be another, etc.) By the end of 1990, more than 20,000 series traded.

As 1990 drew to a close, the exchanges began looking for other revenue opportunities beyond new stocks or indexes. The first of the new products to be added was called LEAPS, Long-Term Equity Anticipation Securities. (Wall Street loves acronyms.) In contrast to then-listed options, which expired in a maximum of nine months, LEAPS initially expire in two years. At the start, LEAPS were available on only 14 blue-chip stocks, but since then, following the pattern of listed options, they have proliferated.

Several other option mutations have been brought out since then, and still others are sure to follow. Although option trading volume has soared, it has not grown as quickly as the number of new series or products, nor of course is trading volume equally distributed between all series or varieties of options. Option activity is measured in terms of daily volume and open interest (the number of open contracts). Trading and open interest in call options is usually two or three times greater than in puts. The relatively few index options account for almost half of all volume and open interest; all equity options account for the balance. As many options series trade infrequently, prices quoted in the newspapers are not always a guide to the price at which an option can actually be bought or sold. The price shown in the newspaper indicates the last trade—which may have occurred early in the day or before a change in the price of the stock.

Index Options

Index options are similar in most respects to equity options, but there are some important differences. Index options are traded on broad-based indexes such as the S&P 500 Index, the New York Stock Exchange Index or the Value Line Composite Index; on intermediate-sized indexes such as the S&P 100; and on narrow-based indexes containing stocks of a single industry. Among the latter are the Computer Technology Index, the Financial News Index, the Gold-Silver Index, etc.

At expiration, index options that are in the money are settled in cash, not stock. The majority of index options are American style, meaning that they can be exercised at any time before expiration, but certain ones, including the S&P 500, Value Line Composite, and Financial News Indexes, are European style and are exercisable only at expiration. (Of course, any option position can be closed out prior to expiration by sale or repurchase.)

PLACING AN ORDER

The Bid/Asked Spread and Liquidity

The bid/asked spread in options can be so wide that it can completely erase the potential profit the option offers. For stocks, bid/asked spreads (the difference between the price buyers bid and the price sellers ask for an issue) typically average 1% to 2%; in options, it averages 15%, wider in equity options, narrower in index options. Of course, the volume of activity in the issue or its liquidity is the key to the breadth of the spread. The greater the volume, the narrower the spread.

The wide spreads can make the least active options appear most favorably priced, but this is often an illusion. Consider an option that last traded at 1 1/8. You would like to sell it at that price. Unfortunately, the last investor was a buyer who paid the "asked" price. The option is quoted 7/8 – 1 1/8. If you want to sell it, you would get only the "bid," 7/8 (22% less).

Prices reported in the newspapers are even less reliable as a guide to where an inactive option will trade. Newspapers show the last trade, which may have occurred hours before the close. If the price of the stock changed, that option price will be out of sync with the stock.

To save time and reduce frustration, except in circumstances that leave no choice, it is wise to confine your interest to the more active issues. Liquidity in options is measured in terms of the number of contracts traded and open interest (the number of open contracts). A more useful measure, you will find, is the dollar value of contracts traded and open interest. After all, 1,000 contracts traded at a sixteenth ($0.0625) represents a market value of only $6,250 whereas 10 contracts traded at $10 have a value of $10,000.

To avoid letting all or most of the profit slip away in the process of establishing an option position, it's necessary to tie the price at which you'll trade the option to the price of the underlying stock. You may not always have the patience to do this if you're in a hurry to close out a position but you should always do it when you open a position. The way to do this is by placing contingent orders as follows:

◆ Buy calls: "Buy March 50 XYZ calls at 3 with the stock 49 1/2 or higher."

◆ Sell calls: "Sell March 50 XYZ calls at 3 with the stock 49 1/2 or lower."

◆ Buy puts: "Buy March 50 XYZ puts at 2 with the stock 49 1/2 or lower."

◆ Sell puts: "Sell March 50 XYZ calls at 2 with the stock 49 1/2 or higher."

Not all brokers will take contingent orders like these, often because they don't know that they can. If your broker won't, select another. NEVER place an opening order for an option without tying it to the price of the stock.

Commissions

A major cost of option trading can be commission charges. Commission charges normally rise more slowly than the value of the trade with a minimum charge being levied no matter how small the trade. Exhibit 1.1 illustrates the commission schedule (in part) for options at one discount broker.

If you bought one option contract at $1 a share, since each contract represents 100 shares, the total value of the trade would be $100. Commissions would add $25, or 25% to the cost. On the other hand, if you sold that contract, instead of pocketing $100, after commissions you'd net $75. Larger orders reduce the impact of commissions. If you

Exhibit 1.1 Sample Commission Schedule

Number of Contracts	1	5	10	1	5	10
Option Price	Commissions			Percentage of Option's Price		
$1	$25.00	$36.38	$46.75	25.0%	7.3%	3.6%
2	25.00	38.50	53.90	12.5%	3.9%	1.9%
3	25.00	39.98	54.50	8.3%	2.7%	1.3%
4	25.00	44.20	59.00	6.3%	2.2%	1.1%
5	25.00	44.70	63.50	5.0%	1.8%	0.9%

bought 10 contracts at $1 a share, a total trade worth $1,000, commissions would add 3.6%. (As a rule of thumb, commissions are double at full-cost brokers.)

While it is tempting to decide after examining this commission schedule that it is advantageous to concentrate in the higher-priced options, you will find that the majority of trading is done in the lowest-priced options trading—at $0.50 or less. There are, however, two lessons to be learned from this schedule:

1. It's necessary to trade in sufficient quantities to insure that commissions don't overwhelm profit opportunities. Commissions of 5% are the maximum you can consider. If you have an active account at a full-cost broker, negotiated rates are possible. The best rates are enjoyed by the most active accounts who trade hundreds of contracts or more at a time.

They are usually charged no more than $0.05 a share, but less on low-priced options.

2. Option orders are executed on the floor of the exchange as matching orders on the other side are received. If you place an order for 100 calls at $0.25 a call, worth $2,500 in total, and only four contracts worth $100 are executed during the day, you'd be charged a minimum commission of $25, which amounts to 25% of the total trade. To avoid that, give your broker additional instructions, as follows:

> Buy (sell) 100 March 70 XYZ calls at $0.25 with the stock at 49 1/2 *all or none* (or *minimum of 50*).

Spreads

Positions such as spreads that combine more than one option (see Chapter 7) should be ordered as a single transaction. Such orders will be executed only if the price relation between the options is preserved.

Consider, for example, a combination position in which you would like to purchase a call selling for $3 a share and sell another at a price of $1 a share. Your net outlay would be $2 a share. If you placed separate orders, however, you might find that the one you hoped to buy was quoted 2 3/4–3 1/4 and the other you hoped to sell was quoted at 7/8–1 1/8. Normally, you must buy at the asked and sell at the bid. If you did this, you'd pay $3.25 for the first and sell the other at $0.88. Instead of a net cost of $2 a share for the position, you'd pay $2.37, an 18.5% premium. That would be the equivalent of paying $118.50

for IBM at a time when it was trading at $100. You can't afford that.

To avoid establishing this position for more than $2 a share, place the order specifying the net debit (or credit, if you were selling the $3 call and buying the $1 call). Instruct your broker to:

> Buy 10 October XYZ calls struck at $30 and sell 10 October XYZ calls struck at $35 for a net debit (excluding commissions) of $2 a share.

Now your order will be executed only on the terms you specified, or better. While there is no guarantee that the broker will be able to execute the order, it will make it easier for the broker to do so. It leaves him free to buy the lower strike at $3.25 and sell the higher at $1.25, or any other combination that nets out to $2.

The Changing Market

Bear in mind, however, that as the stock rises and falls, the change in the value of each option will be different; moreover, price changes are greater as the stock rises than when it falls. Consider the following XYZ calls, for example:

Stock Price	$31	$32	$33
Buy October 30 call	2 3/4	3	3 5/16
Sell October 35 call	7/8	1	1 3/16
Fair Value of Spread	1 7/8	2	2 1/8

As you can see, if the price of the stock fell and your order to buy this spread was executed at $2, you'd pay too much for it. Conversely, if the stock rose and you sold this spread for $2, you'd receive too little for it.

Is a sixteenth or an eighth of a point important? If you were flipping a coin, would you give better than 50-50 odds that the coin would come up heads? Take shorter odds and you might win once or twice or even several times in a row, but eventually you'll come out a loser. The price at which you establish a position establishes the odds of whether you'll make a profit or not.

> In the fall of 1991, shortly after Goldman Sachs marketed PENs, a new security it invented, I expressed dismay that it had been overpriced. Institutional customers, unaware that PENs were actually naked calls (see Chapter 6), had overpaid. A Goldman Sachs executive said, "It may be overpriced, but all we need is a good market to bail them out and the buyers will be happy."

> Unless you're confidant you'll be lucky, you may not be willing to count on a good market to bail you out. If you consistently accept short odds, over time you're going to come up short.

To avoid having an order executed at an unfavorable price if the stock rises or falls, take the following steps:

1. Place day orders. When you trade options, there is only one situation that warrants a "GTC" (good-till-canceled order), and that's when it's time to buy back a short option at expiration.

2. Place contingent orders. For example: "Buy the above bull call spread for a $2 debit with the stock

at $32 or higher," or "sell the spread for a $2 credit with the stock at $32 or lower."

Covered Calls

Covered calls, like spreads, are positions combining two issues and should be ordered as a single transaction. If, for example, you wished to buy 500 shares of XYZ at $32 a share and sell the March 35 call against it for $1 a share, you'd instruct your broker to do the following:

> Buy 500 XYZ common and sell 5 XYZ March 35 calls for a net debit of $31 a share.

Closing Option Positions

The same rules for opening positions apply to closing them. Unlike opening positions, however, you may not have the luxury to wait until prices become acceptable if you are in a hurry to close out a position. Still, there is rarely an urgency to act during the week when the option is about to expire. At that time, you will almost always find that you can close out the position at the tangible value of the option. Place the order as follows:

> Buy (sell) to close 10 XYZ March 35 options at parity.

Generally, the closer to expiration, or the greater the tangible value, the easier it will be to fill such an order. The party on the other side of the contract will normally be equally anxious to close out the contract to avoid the higher commissions that would be incurred if the option is exercised. You may choose to wait until Friday, the day of expiration, to close out your position, though it's wise to act at least a day or two earlier to avoid unexpected hitches.

If you own an in-the-money option, and commissions would cost more than you'll realize on its sale, allow it to expire unexercised. Similarly, if you sold an option that is out of the money, simply let it expire. Note, however, that risk increases very rapidly as the option gets closer and closer to expiration. If, with a few days to go, a small move in the stock could result in a large loss in the option, consider closing it out in advance of expiration.

If you sold an option that's in the money by even a few pennies at expiration, don't take a chance that it won't be exercised. At expiration, options in the money by more than $0.75 that a holder fails to exercise are exercised for him automatically; but even options worth only a few cents might be exercised by a floor broker who pays no commissions.

And now . . .
. . . let's begin examining option strategies that offer above-average returns and others that are guaranteed to lose money in the long run and should be carefully avoided.

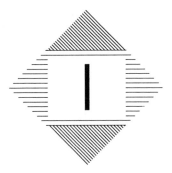

COMMON
MISCONCEPTIONS

When Puts Put It to You

In which we learn that unless you are psychic and can call the market consistently, using puts as insurance to protect stocks from a drop in the market is guaranteed to cost you more than it will save you (though the commission business will earn you the deep-felt gratitude of your broker).

The scene is a meeting of the Association of Individual Investors (an oxymoron that may be an appropriate start for the evening). This evening's seminar is on options. On the panel with me is John Ganzemache, the highly visible head of options marketing for one of the largest retail brokerage networks in the United States and Robert Hochem, one of the most respected names in option theory, listed just south of Fisher Black and Myron Scholes, the two men who created the Black-Scholes Model, which is used as the standard for option evaluation. More about Mr. Hochem in the next chapter.

The first of this evening's presentations was made by John Ganzemache. As head of retail option sales, his income is tied to the volume of option trading at his firm and he's not here altruistically. His topic: Why puts are an excellent means of protecting stock investments from going south. In all fairness, he may be a believer: many of the texts make a similar assertion. Even well-respected Wall Street houses have been heard to urge this strategy on unsuspecting institutional clients.

Let's see how puts work, why that claim is made for them (and why you should avoid that strategy like the plague).

A put is a contract between the buyer of the put and the seller of the put, who is also called the "writer." (Any investor who has a margin account can buy a put, or sell a put or a call.) If you were to buy a put, you'd have the privilege of selling 100 shares of a specified stock at an agreed-upon price to the seller of the put during the period during which the put remained outstanding. For this, you'd pay a fee to the seller called a "premium."

What Mr. Ganzemache is suggesting is that you protect your stock holdings by buying puts. For example, if you held 100 shares of Chase Manhattan stock selling for $20 a share and were concerned that the price might tank, you could buy a put giving you the right to sell that stock at $20 a share. If Chase Manhattan's price were to fall, you could simply exercise your put and sell your stock for the agreed-upon price of $20 a share and you'd come out unscathed. At least that's what he claimed. Let's see if that's really so.

How long is that Chase Manhattan put to run? If you chose a six-month period, that put might cost you about $2 a share. That would give you full insurance for six months. If the stock dropped below $20 during that six-month period, you'd simply exercise your put and sell the stock to the writer for $20 a share. You'd come out whole for the modest cost of only $2 a share. But if the price of the stock went up, you wouldn't use the put; you'd allow it to expire unexercised and keep your stock now worth a lot more.

A pretty good deal! Either way you win. If the price goes up, you keep the stock and enjoy the full appreciation. If the price drops, you get bailed out without a loss. All for the price of $2.

If you think that's a good deal, why not keep that insurance in force not just for 6 months but continually? You'd be able to invest risk free—heads the market goes up and you reap the gain, tails the market goes down and your loss is covered. After all, you have your home insured against fire all the time—not just when you suspect a fire may break out.

But wait. Before you rush out to buy puts to insure your stocks against loss as Mr. Ganzemache recommended, let's look at a few numbers. With Chase Manhattan selling at $20 a share, that "modest" $2 a share for six-month put insurance works out to 10% of the value of the stock. That's equivalent to about 20% a year. Historically, stocks have provided a total return (from price appreciation and dividends) of only about 12% a year. So if you keep put "insurance" in force, on average you'll be in the hole by about 8% a year!

Ha ha! you say, but I'm only going to buy puts when I fear the market is going down. Congratulations! My hat's off to you. You're undoubtedly an expert at forecasting the market. If you can forecast that well, maybe you should buy fire insurance for your home only when you expect there's going to be a fire.

Of course that's ridiculous. You can't forecast when your home will catch fire . . . and unless you're better than 99.99% of the market experts I've met or read over the past 25 years, you can't forecast the market either.[1] Indeed, if you can forecast the market, why buy stocks? You can do a lot better betting on the market itself. Simply buy a call on the S&P 500 Averages whenever you predict the market's going up and you'll make your fortune in no time . . . if you're right. Double up, if you like, buy calls when the market's going to rise and puts when it's going to dive— and you'll get wealthy twice as fast.

So if buying puts is foolish, what should you do? First, recognize that if you buy puts, you are buying an expensive form of insurance. On average, you'll lose capital at the rate of about 8% a year for the period the insurance is in force. That's like owning a $100,000 home and paying $8,000 a year for fire insurance. You can't afford that kind of insurance.

Look at it this way. Suppose you can forecast the market correctly half the time. That is, one out of two times when you think the market will dive and you buy a put, your stock does fall and the put pays off. The other time, whatever you shelled out for the put is wasted. How steep a drop would there have to be on those alternate times when the stock did drop just to let you break even—to cover the cost for the two puts?

---

1 From *The Wall Street Journal,* June 17, 1991: "Seven Common Mistakes Investors Make . . . Thinking You Can Time the Market. Investors continue to attempt to time the stock market, even though every study shows that the chances of doing that successfully are slim . . ."

Let's consider the puts on Chase Manhattan at $2 a share again. If you covered your position twice and one of those times the stock went down and the other it didn't, you'd have coughed up $4 a share. To recover that cost, the stock would have to fall 4 points. Since the stock was at $20, that's a drop of 20%. Add in commissions and that brings the decline needed to break even to 22%—simply to cover your costs.

A 22% decline. How often does that occur? If we looked at the market overall, with the Dow Jones Industrial Average at 3,000, a 22% decline would be the equivalent of 660 points. Of course, individual stocks are more volatile. Still, how many times in your experience has the market declined 660 points in six months?

But that's not the worst of it. Even if there was a 22% decline, the odds are against you; it's unlikely that you will cover your costs! Remember, your put expires in six months. If the stock sinks, are you going to exercise your put if it still has several weeks or months before it expires? Hardly. After all, you're guaranteed at least $20 a share up until the put's expiration. So why exercise prematurely? You can't do worse if you wait but you could do better. It could turn around and shoot up before the put expired. You're in a no-lose situation. So, though you can exercise your put at any time during the six months, the only time you're really likely to exercise it is just before it expires . . . and only if Chase Manhattan is down more than 22% at that precise instant in time will buying the put have paid off for you.

IS THERE A BETTER WAY?

Certainly. One way is to sit tight. Just because you're skittish doesn't mean the market's going straight to zero. If you can't forecast the market, when it looks the darkest to you it is just as likely to rise as to fall.

Another alternative, of course, is to sell your stock and switch into money market instruments—CDs, T-bills, etc. But that may not be right for you if you'll be subject to a large tax bite—or if you plan to buy back the stock, for commissions and transaction costs can eat you up. Even then, you have to be exceptionally clairvoyant: assuming the market continues to provide an average annual return from appreciation and dividends of about 12% a year over time, if you were to switch into the market when you forecast the market was going to rise and switch out when you forecast it was going to fall, under most any reasonable assumption you might make about market fluctuations, interest rates available on alternate investments, and commission charges, you'd have to be right more than 75% of the time to beat a strategy of continually remaining 100% invested!

But there are at least three other strategies that make sense. One of the best is writing covered calls against your stock holdings. Covered call writing reduces your risk much like buying a put, but instead of winding up costing you money and cutting your returns over time, it brings in income and typically enhances your returns. This is discussed in greater detail in a later chapter.

If your goal is to protect an entire portfolio rather than a single stock, you might prefer a strategy I favor, which I call "covered portfolio writing." Writing futures or options against one of the market indexes is also an effective way of adding income as you protect your portfolio. Both of these strategies are discussed later in this book, too.

SUMMING UP

Puts are an extremely costly way to get peace of mind when used as insurance for individual stocks. The average stock provides a return of about 12% a year; the average put premium runs 20% a year.

After saying all this, it might seem inconsistent to state that there can be a place for puts in a portfolio. A small amount of puts (about 4%) married to a diversified stock portfolio can, if intelligently selected, add about 5% a year to the stock returns over a very long span and, by moving contrary to the market, slightly reduce the volatility and so enhance the reward/risk ratio. The puts, however, are selected independently of the stocks held (and not necessarily written against those stocks), much on the order of covered portfolio writing discussed in a later chapter.

But other strategies have had better success, particularly covered call writing and covered portfolio writing, both of which, over the long run, have generated better total returns with lower volatility and with fewer periods of losses.

Implied Future Volatility

Although we may learn by processing an option through our handy-dandy Black-Scholes model how volatile other option traders think the underlying stock will be in the future, unless we make similar calculations for virtually every option, our effort was more for fun (and our personal edification) than for profit . . . for there is a logical relationship between the prices of all options much as if they were set out on a giant checkerboard—and when one shifts position, we can be reasonably sure that opportunity is knocking only if others haven't shifted with it. When prices of all options on a stock—or on all stocks—have shifted in tandem, it may signal that it isn't opportunity that is knocking, but that others have better information

*about that stock, or the forces that drive market prices,
than you do.*

Speaker No. 2 on the panel with me at the Association of
Independent Investors was Robert Hochem, introduced to
you in Chapter 2. As noted, Hochem, a man well known in
the lore of options theory, was not quite Black or Scholes,
but no shlump either. (Fisher Black and Myron Scholes col-
laborated on the development of the mathematical formula
that is used widely for valuing options; it's as well known
in the field of option theory as the Dow Jones Industrial
Average is in the stock market. Although the Black-Scholes
model is not the last word in option valuation any more
than the Dow Jones Average is the last word in the valuation of the market, out of custom, both have come into
generic use.)

Mr. Hochem's topic that night was "Using Implied Future Volatility to Achieve Obscene Wealth and Absolute
Happiness." You may be wondering what implied future
volatility is and how it relates to option trading. That's
what Mr. Hochem promised to tell this group of retirees
and hopeful investors.

"Ask yourself," Hochem said, "how do you decide if
the price of an option is low so that you should snap up
the bargain, or if it's being offered at boutique prices and
you should sell! sell! sell! For example, can you say for sure
what a six-month call on Compaq Computer is worth if
Compaq stock is at $35?"

A call on Compaq (as you know) gives you the right to
buy 100 shares of Compaq at an agreed-upon price
(which is also known as the strike or exercise price). In
this case, the option is to run six months. In order to

place a value on the call, however, we must know other things. One of those is the exercise price. If it were exercisable at $30 a share and Compaq was trading at $35 in the market, you could immediately exercise the call—pay $30 a share for the stock—turn around and sell it for $35, and pocket a $5 a share profit. That call, then, would have an intrinsic or "tangible" value of $5 a share. You'd have to pay at least that and probably a whole lot more.

Of course, you need more information. How soon does the call expire? If it's just about to expire, it's worth no more than its tangible value. But if it has several months to run, it's worth more. Clearly, the longer the option has to run, the more it's worth.

Those are the three basics: stock price, strike price, and time to expiration. But there are other factors that determine whether that call is a bargain or a bomb. High on the list—and the one Mr. Hochem came to *verdreht your kopf* about is volatility. How volatile is Compaq stock? Is it likely to shoot up? If it was highly stable, you wouldn't want to pay much more for it than its tangible value. But if the stock was highly volatile and likely to jump in price, that call could soar in value and it would be worth a lot more.

But do you really want to know how volatile the stock has been, or do you want to know how volatile it will be? Obviously, it's how volatile it will be, Mr. Hochem confided to the uninitiated in the audience.

Before we continue, let's note that the value of a call depends to a minor extent on two other factors, the dividend paid on the underlying stock and the "risk-free rate" of interest, the amount you could earn without risk by buying Treasury bills or in the bank. To summarize, then, the value of an option depends on five factors:

A. The price at which it exercises compared to the price of the stock.

B. The time to expiration.

C. The risk-free interest rate.

D. The dividend paid by the stock.

E. The future volatility of the stock.

Of course, no one can tell how volatile a stock will be in the future. But, as Hochem told the audience, you can tell how volatile other option traders expect it to be. Sound extrasensory? It's really rather simple, he confided with a look that promised secrets to riches that the audience was longing to learn.

"It's rather simple," Hochem repeated, "with the aid of the Black-Scholes model or, even better, with the use of my 'Hochem' model which," he suggested, careful to suppress any modesty, false or otherwise, "is vastly superior." The Black-Scholes model? You'll remember that I started this chapter by mentioning the Black-Scholes model, a model used to derive the value of options via a mathematical formula. By feeding in the five factors listed above, the model arrives at a fair value for an option. Essentially it says:

Price of Option = A + B + C + D + E

If you'll refer back to the five factors on that list, you'll notice that four of the five are known. Only E, the future volatility of the stock, isn't known. If we want to derive a price for the option we can estimate it, *or instead we can input the price of the option and solve for E.* After all, the price at which the option is trading is based on how volatile option traders expect the stock to be. So when we solve the equation for the unknown factor "E" using the price of the option, we learn how volatile others expect the stock to be in the future. We call this the stock's "implied" future volatility since this volatility is *implied* by the price of the option.

So, Mr. Hochem, how does this make us rich? Many in the audience read the basic text, too. No secrets here yet.

Unruffled, Mr. Hochem continued. "When exciting news breaks, investors look for the stock's volatility to rise and price its options accordingly. If the expected change in volatility is great, the price change in its option will be great, too. But is that change justified? Or will the volatility revert to the prior volatility—which is what normally happens? By comparing the volatility implied by the option's price to the stock's historic volatility, we can select the volatility that allows us to determine the 'correct' price for the option and for uncovering whopping profit opportunities."

And saying this, Mr. Hochem's eyelids dipped, his head bowed ever so slightly, and a gesture not unlike one of benediction crept across his countenance. A few in the audience, scatterings here and there, applauded uncertainly. Before Mr. Hochem lifted his eyelids to accept the accolades, a puzzled voice raised above the shuffling of chairs. "Yes, but how does that help? How do we decide whether to use the 'implied future volatility,' the historic volatility, or some figure between the two?"

"Ah," responded Mr. Hochem, "that is the question!"

Thank you Mr. Hochem. In the course of your 30-minute presentation, you have "enlightened" us by showing that the price of an option depends on the future volatility of the stock, and that if we knew it, we'd become filthy rich. You have further explained that though we (obviously) can't know how volatile the stock will be in the future, you say we can discover how volatile others guess it will be by a simple mathematical test. Then we have our choice: we can trade the option based on that volatility—or we can base it on the stock's historic volatility. That advice falls into the category of help we gave to only our closest pals in school: If you're stuck, take a guess at the answer and divide by two. That way you'll make half the error.

In fact, Hochem has told us less than that. What he failed to mention is that there are often 20 or more options on any stock, and if you run each through the Black-Scholes model, you'll probably come up with 20 different "implied future volatilities." It would be just your luck to find that the future volatility implied by the option you want to trade is different from the future volatility implied by all the others. What a dilemma. Before you trade an option, you darned well better test each of the options on that stock—and then guess which one is right.

Ah, if it were only so easy even then. What if investors have taken a fresh view of the future volatility of the *entire market* but haven't yet focused on the options of your stock. Before you trade that option, then, don't you want to get a handle on market "sentiment" by testing a cross section of options on other stocks? Indeed, you have plenty to choose from: over 20,000 listed options trade on over 600 stocks, a number that is growing daily.

So, Mr. Hochem, the poor shnook who came to hear this advice should be grateful? Tell it like it is, sir . . .

If, as we know, the volatility of a stock remains relatively constant over periods of three years or more, though it may rise or fall temporarily, it is likely to revert to the norm. Similarly, the market's volatility may rise or fall, temporarily carrying stocks with it, then revert to the norm.

Can we turn this knowledge into cash? Yes, think of options set out on a huge checkerboard, with each option in its proper place relative to all others. If the price of one option moves out of line with others on the same stock, it's obviously mispriced and presents an opportunity to cash in. If the prices of all options on a single stock get out of line, something's afoot. Maybe a rumor, maybe the insiders know something you don't. Though it's probable those options will move back into line, holding them can be messy if the rumors prove true, or even if they don't before those options—or your pocketbook—has run out. Finally, if the prices of *all* options get out of line, it's clear that investors are jittery. That rarely lasts very long, so take the long view.

And how do you keep track of each option in this matrix? The Black-Scholes model or others will help. It's clear, however, that the best opportunities will be discovered by investors capable of the broadest coverage, or who subscribe to a service, such as the one I created at Value Line.

Do many opportunities arise? Absolutely. Option prices are not terribly efficient—and with good reason. Up to 50% of all option trading is accounted for by a handful of options on the popular indexes, such as the S&P 500 index. But for more than 19,000 equity options, less than half trade on any given day. And where trading is light, the spread between the bid and the asked price can be enormous. Indeed, whereas the average bid/asked spread for New York Stock Exchange stocks is less than 2%, it's 15% for options. But that's the *average.* Spreads for options of up to 100% are not all that rare. An option that last traded at $.50 might next be quoted $.25/$.75.

Is this a reason to stay away? Not at all. When trading is light and spreads are large, broad inefficiencies pop up that alert traders can take advantage of. You do, however, need a high-speed computer or a service that culls out these options for you.

SUMMING UP

The use of the Black-Scholes (or other such mathematical) model to look at a single individual option is of limited value. Indeed, when an institutional trader at Merrill Lynch, present at the introduction of Merrill's "Blumberg" model, perhaps the most sophisticated such model ever constructed, with more bells and whistles than can be found at Disneyland, was asked what he does if the market price is different than the price indicated by the model, he replied: "I go with the market."

There is no "right" price for an individual option. It must be priced in relation to the prices of other options on the same stock, options on other stocks, and, ultimately, to returns available elsewhere on other kinds of investments. Thus, the proper evaluation of one option can best be determined with the aid of a matrix that defines each option's proper place within it and so identifies those options or groups of options that are overpriced or underpriced and by how much. In such a model, calculations of implied future relative volatility are of limited use, for the model tunes into the market pragmatically rather than through calculations designed to intuit mystically a stock's future volatility.

For those who wish to use Value Line Options' estimates of future volatilities, simply divide Value Line's estimate of an option's relative volatility by its estimate of the option's leverage. (Relative volatility is the volatility of a stock or other instrument compared to the average volatility of all stocks. A relative volatility of 150% indicates that the instrument is 50% more volatile than the average stock, etc. Value Line's estimate of the option's leverage is shown in the publication as "Current Leverage" for a 10% rise or a 10% fall in the stock. For example, if the option's relative volatility was 1,200%, and its upside leverage was 80%, (for a 10% rise in the stock)—indicating that it was expected to rise eight times faster than the stock—and its downside leverage was 4, (i.e., 40% for a 10% drop in the stock) simply divide the 1,200% relative volatility of the option by the average leverage, 6. Value Line's estimate of the future volatility of the stock would be 200%. As relative volatilities and leverage figures are rounded, take an average of several options on the same stock.)

A "Guaranteed" Return

It is here that we take an in-depth look at a portfolio "insurance" scheme, this one created by two business school professors, a scheme so exciting it was published in not one, but two leading investment journals . . . a scheme that guaranteed profits if the market fell without sacrificing profits if it rose . . . a scheme as tempting as the portfolio insurance gambits that swept into popularity in early 1987 and which left money managers weeping when the market crashed . . . and we discover that, undaunted, money managers adopted still another portfolio insurance scheme in 1991 in an attempt to safeguard $25 billion of equities. And we learn, perhaps, a little to our delight, that even the expert fund managers haven't *lost their belief in Santa Claus . . . but that if a scheme seems to good to be true, it usually is.*

One of the more amusing academic proposals I've come across in my career was originally published in the prestigious *Financial Analysts Journal,* a publication that purports to be to the financial world what the *New England Journal of Medicine* is to the world of medicine. The articles published in the *Financial Analysts Journal* are generally so technical and chock full of arcane statistics and mathematics that relatively few readers—despite the plethora of advanced degrees analysts have to their credit—are likely to be capable of authenticating the procedures let alone the conclusions described in them. So it is logical that the *Journal's* board of editors includes a long slate of legendary names, a Who's Who of quantitative analysts in the academic and institutional world of stock evaluation. Do these renowned experts lend their names to the Journal to add further luster to their prestige or do they actually have a function on the publication? Several articles that have appeared in those august pages leaves one to wonder.

One such article described a strategy that the author had devised to enable investors to get the full benefit of any rise in the value of their portfolios with no risk of loss if their stocks went down . . . in fact, with a guarantee of a positive return even if the stocks went down. Little wonder that it was later reprinted in part in the *Journal of the Association of Independent Investors,* and that article, in turn, was later excerpted by *The Wall Street Journal.* The author was a professor of business at one of the Southeastern universities. It would be a kindness not to mention his name.

The scheme he proposed came at a time when portfolio "insurance" was a hot idea. In essence, his was a simple plan, though of course in the tradition of these things, it was written up at some length with elaborate documentation. But with the trappings removed, the proposal called for the purchase of a put on the entire portfolio struck at a price above the market.

The scheme went like this: You hold a diversified portfolio worth, say for simplicity, $100. To guarantee a profit, you buy a put exercisable above the market—say at 5% above the market—thus, a put exercisable at $105. If the market fails to go up, you exercise your put and receive $105 for your holdings. If the market and your holdings go up more than that, you let the put expire unused. So if the market goes up, you get the full benefit of the market's rise, but if it doesn't go up, you exercise your put and realize a 5% profit. Dividend income would come in addition.

A win-win strategy.

What could go wrong? Nothing!

Indeed, it seemed nothing could go wrong! That may be why it got past a lot of editors. For nothing could go wrong—*assuming you could set up this in the first place.* That's what they missed. This scheme simply couldn't be set up. Why? Follow along with me.

Let's assume, for example, that you held a widely diversified portfolio of stocks worth, in total, $100, whose makeup exactly mirrored the S&P Averages. In other words, your equity has a value of $100. To "guarantee" yourself a minimum return of 5%, you buy a one-year put (on the equivalent of the S&P 500 Averages) exercisable at $105. Thus, one year from now, if your holdings are worth less than $105, you exercise your put, sell your holdings, and pocket $105. You have realized your objective of earning a minimum 5% return. On the other hand, if your holdings are worth more than $105, you let the put expire unused and come away with a higher return.

Let's go back to the beginning of the year now and follow the mechanics of this transaction step by step. You have a portfolio of stocks worth $100 and buy a put on those stocks at $105. But wait—how much will that put cost?

A put at $105 with the stock at $100 is $5 in the money. That is, it has a tangible or intrinsic value of $5. You could immediately exercise that put, sell your stock for $105, and pocket the $5 difference between what you got for the put and the value of your stock. That put, then, would sell for a minimum of $5. In addition, you'd pay for the "time premium," an additional amount over the tangible value which is recompense to the seller for providing that option for the period of time it would run. A one-year at-the-money put (an at-the-money put on a $100 portfolio would be exercisable at $100) typically commands a time premium of 16%. Thus, a one-year put struck at $100 would cost you $16. If it were exercisable at $105, the time premium would be slightly less but you'd have to ante up the $5 tangible value. Therefore, a put exercisable at $105 would probably cost $20.

So suppose you found someone willing to sell you a one-year put on your $100 portfolio for $20. Where will you get $20 to pay for it? If you take it out of your pocket, your investment is no longer $100 but $120, so if all you're guaranteed is $105, where's the guaranteed profit? You could wind up with a loss unless your portfolio rose at least 20% (to $120) by the end of the year. Even then you'd only break even.

If, instead, you liquidate part of your portfolio to pay for the put, your holdings will no longer be worth $100, they'd be worth only $80. But in that case, a put at $105 would no longer be $5 in the money. It would be $25 in the money (!) and so it would cost you more than $25. In this case you'd have to liquidate still more of your portfolio to pay for it, which would reduce the value of your portfolio still further, which would raise the tangible value of the put still more, and so you'd have to liquidate still more of your portfolio to pay for it . . . etc., etc., ad infinitum.

I wrote to the Journal suggesting that the scheme was redolent of Ponzi and pointed out why. The letter was forwarded to the author who called me to advise that I simply didn't understand the scheme, that if the mathematics didn't work at $105, you would simply buy a put at a higher price! When I explained how the same conditions would apply, he promised to work out the numbers and get back to me. Perhaps one day he will.

How sad. If a scheme seems to good to be true, it almost always turns out so.

PERCS: The Covered Call That Lost Its Birthright

It is here we learn that a rose is no longer a rose . . . at least not since 1991, for derivatives—which once were simply options, warrants, and convertibles—have mutated in the laboratories of creative investment bankers. Today, the investor who buys an issue that is represented to be a rose without looking closely may find he owns something with a less attractive aroma . . . for minor changes in terms are turning once attractive issues into securities of substantially lesser value. Among those recently brought to market are PERCS and MCPDPS. Represented to be "convertibles," they are, in fact, nothing of the sort.

There are few skeptics among investors. Let someone paint a picture of obscene profits, and even the professionals who should know better will beg for an opportunity to invest, price no object. Said one professional at a 1991 Goldman Sachs convertibles conference, "I don't care if a convertible is overpriced. As long as I like the underlying stock, I'll buy it." This is an attitude that has been coming back into vogue lately as stocks climb to dizzy heights. It was last prevalent back in the late 1960s when prices were running wild. One securities analyst (I won't name him and embarrass him, he's still around and somewhat less optimistic) urged me to buy stock in a tiny company, arguing "Forget about its sky-high price/earnings multiple . . . . As long as you know you can make a 50% profit on a run up in the stock in a few months, what's the difference what price you pay for it?"

Newcomers to the business who lack perspective are particularly prone to optimism, like the one who catapulted into my office two weeks after he was hired almost swooning, "I'm going to make over 100% a year on my money!" he exclaimed. (Wow! I wondered greedily, what's his secret?) "I began investing last week," he continued, "and my stocks are up over 1%! That compounds to over 100% a year!" Zowie! He soon found another line of work.

GETTING PERKY

On Wall Street, a good story, or it seems even a good acronym, can persuade money managers to line up cash in hand. This was the case when General Motors PERCS were brought to market. A new invention of Morgan Stanley (standing for Preferred Equity Redemption Cumulative

Stock), the issue quickly separated fund managers from $600 million dollars. What does that mouthful mean? Who knows? Even the underwriter didn't know when I asked. All most money managers knew for certain was that General Motors wanted to raise more than a half billion dollars selling an issue Morgan Stanley said was a preferred stock and convertible. As you'll see, in fact, it wasn't either.

For the underwriting community, a successful underwriting offers follow-on benefits; similar issues can later be successfully marketed even if they contain less attractive terms or are obligations of poorer quality companies. And so it was that within weeks, Merrill Lynch launched its own version of GM's PERCS, which it called Mandatory Conversion Premium Dividend Preferred Stock—an acronym about which it felt strongly enough to copyright. (Thus, the investment community came to be treated to a derivative of a derivative, Merrill Lynch's version of Morgan Stanley's version of a convertible preferred stock.)

I missed the pitch for the GM PERCS but attended the luncheon (called "road show" appropriately enough) for the MCPDPS. Merrill Lynch's MCPDPS raised $80 million for Broad, Inc. It was a highly successful deal; Merrill Lynch has a large retail sales force that can make almost any deal a success. It wasn't true, as some wags suggested, that the Broad's MCPDPS raised less money than GM's PERCS because MCPDPS is harder to pronounce.

The question arises, naturally, whether these underwritings would have been equally successful if, rather than being marketed as convertible preferred stocks, they had been described more accurately as what they really were. While we cannot know, we do know that there is a segment of the institutional investment community that specializes in buying convertibles who were invited to the presentations. Did those people who bought realize that they were not buying convertible preferred stocks at all, that they were actually buying covered calls?

PERCS VERSUS CONVERTIBLES

Before we see why these were not convertibles but rather covered calls, we should agree on some common definitions. The word "convertible" may seem to include any security that converts into another, but to the people who specialize in convertibles, it has a specific definition. By common acceptance, a "convertible" is a generic name for a type of security that is (1) exchangeable for another security or for cash, (2) is convertible solely at the discretion of the holder, and (3) is a bond or preferred stock. If one of these three conditions is not present, then it is not a "convertible" in the accepted sense. For example, an option and a warrant are both (1) exchangeable and (2) exchangeable at the discretion of the holder, but because they are not (3) bonds or preferred stocks they are not "convertibles."

PERCS and MCPDPS also failed to fulfill at least one, or perhaps two, requirements. In their case, convertibility was not at the discretion of the holder but at the discretion of the company. The holder has no say in the matter. The company may convert these issues at any time before the end of three years; if it doesn't, it is required to do so at the end of three years. The fact that the company must convert these issues into common stock suggests that a second condition generic to a convertible is not met: since investors must ultimately receive common stock, rather than a bond or preferred stock, it appears that what they really bought was common stock.

WHY A COVERED CALL?

Although it is clear then that PERCS and MCPDPS are not true "convertibles," that doesn't necessarily make them covered calls. What does make them covered calls is another singularity in their terms. Whereas "convertibles" convert into a fixed number of shares, the number of shares that PERCS and MCPDPSs convert into shrinks if the price of the stock rises. Thus, unlike convertibles, which participate fully in a rise in the stock, these issues share in any appreciation to only a small extent. Consider the difference. A convertible exchangeable for one share of common has a value on conversion of $20 when the common is $20; that value rises to $40 if the common rises to $40. But PERCS and MCPDPS convert into fewer shares as the stock rises so that their value on conversion can never rise more than 50%. If the stock is $20 or less, for example, if converted by the company, holders would get one share of common; at higher prices, the number of shares is reduced so that the value shareholders receive is capped at $20. Were the stock to rise to $30, holders would receive two-thirds of a share; at $40, they'd receive one-half share, etc.

If that wasn't bad enough, holders are unlikely to receive even that. The fraction of a share that is distributed is further reduced by dividends paid during the entire holding period prior to conversion. In the case of MCPDPS, for example, the dividend is $1.15 a year. Thus, if converted after two years, holders would actually receive stock worth a maximum of only $17.70, i.e., the $20 cap less two year's worth of dividends.

This, of course, still doesn't demonstrate that PERCS and MCPDPS are covered calls. That becomes clear when we compare their profit/loss profiles at expiration. Consider Broad's MCPDPS, which initially sold for $13 a share when the common stock also was $13 a share. The maximum value holders of MCPDPS could receive after three years was $21.02—$17.57 in stock plus dividends worth $3.45 ($1.15 a year). Here's how holders would fare for various prices of the stock:

STOCK PRICE	$6	$8	$10	$12	$14	$16	$18	$20	$22	$24
MCPDPS	6.00	8.00	10.00	12.00	14.00	16.00	17.57	17.57	17.57	17.57
Dividends	3.45	3.45	3.45	3.45	3.45	3.45	3.45	3.45	3.45	3.45
Profit/Loss	**-3.55**	**-1.55**	**0.45**	**2.45**	**4.45**	**6.45**	**8.02**	**8.02**	**8.02**	**8.02**

Compare that to the profit/loss profile of a covered call position in which an investor bought the stock initially for $13 a share and sold a three-year call against it with an exercise price of $17.57 for $3.45 a share.

Covered Call

STOCK PRICE	$6	$8	$10	$12	$14	$16	$18	$20	$22	$24
Stock	6.00	8.00	10.00	12.00	14.00	16.00	18.00	20.00	22.00	24.00
Call	3.45	3.45	3.45	3.45	3.45	3.45	3.02	1.02	-0.98	-2.98
Profit/Loss	**-3.55**	**-1.55**	**0.45**	**2.45**	**4.45**	**6.45**	**8.02**	**8.02**	**8.02**	**8.02**

Notice that the profit/loss profiles of the covered call and the MCPDPS are identical. Both are a far cry from what the profit/loss profile of a true "convertible" would look like, which appears below:

Convertible (Investment Value: $13)

STOCK PRICE	$6	$8	$10	$12	$14	$16	$18	$20	$22	$24
Convertible	13.00	13.00	13.00	13.00	14.00	16.00	18.00	20.00	22.00	24.00
Dividend	3.45	3.45	3.45	3.45	3.45	3.45	3.45	3.45	3.45	3.45
Profit/Loss	**3.45**	**3.45**	**3.45**	**3.45**	**4.45**	**6.45**	**8.45**	**10.45**	**12.45**	**14.45**

This profile is of a convertible preferred stock paying an annual dividend of $1.15, which Broad could have issued in place of the MCPDPS. Notice that unlike the MCPDPS, even if the common stock dropped below $13, the convertible would hold its value. That's because with a dividend of $1.15 a year, the preferred would have an "investment value" of $13, the amount investors would pay for this income-paying instrument even if it was not convertible. This investment value acts as a floor under the price of a convertible, enabling it to retain its value even if the price of the stock falls. On the upside, however, its value is not "capped" but rises with the price of the stock.

As you can see, unlike the MCPDPS, which offers a maximum profit of $8.02 but which exposes the holder to increasing losses if the stock declines, a true convertible delivers increasing profits as the stock rises but its downside risk is limited by its investment value.

WERE THE BROAD MCPDPS WORTH THE PRICE?

Now that we have identified that the Broad MCPDPS were really covered calls, we can evaluate them appropriately with standard tools to determine whether they were worth what they cost. To begin, we see that we purchased stock for $13 a share. The premium we received for the call we "sold" against it can be considered to be the difference in the dividends that will be paid on this issue over what we'd receive holding the common, or $3.45 a share. The Black-Scholes model says this call was worth $3.40 a share, a nickel less. But the dividend is received over three years, so its "present value" is just $3.00. Thus, buyers of the Broad,

Inc. preferred were short-changed by $0.40 a share. That may not seem much, but if the average buyer bought 250,000 shares, he overpaid $100,000; that's not small change, even for an institution. For the $80 million issue in total, buyers were overcharged by $2.5 million. Apparently, these emptors weren't caveating.

(*Note:* Experienced investors will undoubtedly notice slight differences between genuine covered calls and convertibles and the examples illustrated here. Most obvious is the fact that a true "convertible" would sell at a premium over its $13 conversion value. Buyers, then, might pay another $2.50, or $15.50 rather than $13. This would reduce the profit the convertible would throw off by $2.50, but would otherwise not alter the comparison. In fact, Broad's MCPDPS were poor relations of even a covered call position, as you'll see.)

THE COVERED CALL THAT LOST ITS BIRTHRIGHT

Clearly, investors who bought PERCS or MCPDPS thinking they were getting a convertible were snookered. Sadly, what they received weren't even authentic covered calls but a cheap imitation. For hidden in the "red herring," as the prospectus that contains a legal description of new issues is aptly known, were covenants suggesting that these issues were born on what used to be called the wrong side of the blanket.

Before taking a look at these covenants, it would be instructive for those not familiar with how new issues are marketed to follow along with the process. Once the deal is put together, the architect, a biggie of the underwriter's, teams up with the sales force to escort the chief executives of the issuing company on a whirlwind cross-country marathon of breakfasts and lunches. All have a financial interest in the success of the deal. After hitting the poshest hotels of the major money markets, their dog and pony show usually winds up at New York's Waldorf or Helmsley Palace. There, after a serving of chicken au fou-ey (isn't chicken on the endangered species list yet?), the chairman makes a speech. Stripped of its nonessentials, he says: "My company is great, it is **very** great, it is *extremely* great! . . . and it's going to get greater, yet!"

But why, asks an innocent in the audience, have you lost money in three out of the last four years? "Ah," the chairman explains, "that was before we reorganized and changed our operating philosophy."

When Merrill Lynch has been the underwriter, a four-color handout has been on the table at every place, gazing up at each money manager. It described, luridly, the returns buyers would enjoy when the stock soars. Nothing of this sort would be permitted in any legal document. Does this handout titillate the fancy of hard-bitten fund managers? Ask Merrill Lynch. Evidently it does, for clearly only a handful wade through 150 pages of difficult-to-understand small print in the prospectus to ferret out the terms of the deal after Merrill Lynch, later in the presentation, takes them through its breathtaking handout line by line. After viewing those charts there, who would be skeptical enough to consider that the stock might go down instead of up, a risk the handout somehow failed to mention. But there was a greater risk hidden in that 150-page prospectus that most investors would miss, even with arduous digging.

Can you decipher this? It can be found on page 18, paragraph 2 of the Broad, Inc. prospectus:

The "Notice Date" with respect to any notice given by the Company in connection with a call or conversion of the Series A Shares means the earlier of the commencement of the mailing of such notice to the holders of Series A Shares or the date such notice is first published in accordance with "Notices to Holders of Series A Shares" below. The "Current Market Price" per share of Common Stock on any date of determination means the average of the daily closing prices on the New York Stock Exchange for the five consecutive trading days ending on and including such date of determination (appropriately adjusted to reflect the occurrence during such five-day period of any event that results in an adjustment of the Common Equivalent Rate); *provided, however,* that if the closing price of the Common Stock on the New York Stock Exchange on the trading day next following such five-day period (the "net-day closing price") is less than 95% of said average closing price, then the Current Market Price per share of Common Stock on such date of determination will be the next-day closing price. Because the price of Common Stock is subject to market fluctuation, it is possible that the next-day closing price could be significantly less than such five-day average.

If you have trouble understanding that, so too did a Merrill Lynch exec. What it says—at least what the two of us, after studying it, believed it says—is that if called, the number of shares of common stock a holder of the Broad, Inc. MCPDPS would receive would be based on the average price of the stock during the five days immediately preceding the call, but that if the price on the sixth day is less than 95% of that average, the number would be based on the price on the sixth day.

THE DEBASING OF THE COVERED CALL

As Gertrude S. might have said, a rose is a rose, but this covered call is beginning to smell. Consider the following:

1. If PERCS or MCPDPS are converted, the number of shares common holders would receive depends on the price of the stock at time of conversion. The higher the price, the fewer the shares. Holders should anticipate, then, that when bad news is in the offing and the company believes its stock will tank, these issues will be converted leaving holders scrambling to dump the common they receive on the market. This is a disadvantage covered call writers don't face, for buyers of calls don't have inside information and so aren't likely to exercise at the most disadvantageous time for the writer.

2. Broad, Inc. has the privilege of converting the preferred based on the price of its stock over the four previous days. If it called the issue after its stock began slipping, the number of shares holders would receive would be based on the higher stock prices that no longer existed so the value of stock holders would wind up with would be less than they were entitled to. But that loss could prove minor. With the stock dropping and holders of $80 million of MCPDPS shares rushing to jump ship like passengers on the Titanic, the market value of their holding could be decimated by the time they found buyers. That's not a problem covered option writers normally face, either.

(*Note:* MCPDPS holders have some small protection in case of a catastrophe. If the price of the stock on the day the company converts is less than 95% of the average price of the prior four days, the issue is converted at the price that day. That's less protection than it might seem, however. Under the terms, if called, the maximum profit a holder is entitled to is 50%. A little figuring will show you that if you received 95% of the price that would result in a 50% profit, your profit could be cut not 5%, but 17%. (How many readers of the prospectus made that calculation? Indeed, how many read the prospectus, at all?)

3. There's another fillip in the call provisions that is even more awkward. If a true "convertible" is called, the holder, not the company, decides whether to convert or not. If he chooses to, the holder may simply allow the issue to be redeemed, in which case he gets paid off in cash. If called, holders normally receive 30 days advance notice. During that period, if the stock drops, it is the company—not the holder—that is at risk. That's because a company normally calls a convertible to force conversion into common stock, not to redeem it for cash. If the stock drops during the 30-day waiting period and the conversion value falls below the call price, the holder will take the cash rather than convert into stock, so the company would find itself in the uncomfortable position of having to ante up cash. Thus, companies rarely call a convertible if they anticipate the stock will drop.

4. Even the "bright" side isn't so bright. The stock has soared, you're sitting with a paper 50% profit early

on, and are ready to cash out. Where will you find a buyer? You're in a no-win position. The PERCS/ MCPDPS can't go any higher (you'd get fewer shares if the stock went higher), but they can go down! Who'd buy an issue that can go down but not up? In real life, when the underlying stock of an issue similar to this rose 50%, the issue sold at a 20% discount, shrinking the expected 50% profit to just 20%! That, too, is a problem covered call writers don't face for the stock and the call can each be traded separately, so either can normally be closed out at a fair price.

AFTER NOTE

The GM PERCS, underwritten by Goldman Sachs, on which the Broad, Inc. issue was patterned, was of slightly better vintage. The conversion rate was based not on the price of the stock during the five days before the call, but on the price of the stock on the day of the call. Of course, this would not insure that a holder could cash out at that price, but at least it didn't tilt the odds against the buyer so egregiously. This was not the first time that underwriters debased an issue that had proven successful in its original version. Zero-coupon convertibles followed this same pattern. But that's another story.

HOW TO AVOID GETTING SNOOKERED

It is often quite difficult to be certain, even after careful inspection, how an issue with unfamiliar terms should be evaluated. Even a complex model such as Bloomberg, or others with which you may be familiar, may not have the capability to evaluate all provisions of unique issues, or it may not be clear exactly how the information about the issue should be input to allow the model to evaluate it correctly. There are, however, two things that can be done to get a clearer picture of such issues.

First, read the prospectus carefully. If any of the language or the intent seems obfuscated or unclear, get a lucid explanation from the underwriter, the company, or, if necessary, legal counsel. Read the footnotes with particular care. It is there, often, that the most important features of the issue, or information regarding the company, can be found. It is dangerous to depend on oral assurances that can contain advertent or inadvertent errors. The prospectus is a legal document cleared by the SEC.

Second, construct a profile of the issue similar to the one in this chapter. The additional effort is well worth the price, for nothing so graphically illustrates the potential rewards and risks. In my experience, one picture literally enables a potential buyer to select a rose and avoid issues of less attractive aroma.

PENs: The "Convertible" Bond the Federal Drug Administration Didn't Approve

Here, yet, is another of the clever new derivatives marketed as convertibles. The six-year United Technologies "convertible bond" created by Goldman Sachs pays no interest and offers no return other than a play on the Pharmaceutical/Health Care Index. Marketed as a convertible bond, how many realized that what they had really bought was a naked call!

To those who were born believing that gilt-edge firms are above the sharp practices of some Wall Street houses, it often comes as a shock when you find that even your heroes are not above cutting corners for the sake of a paltry million bucks, or two, or three.

An underwriter's overriding ambition is to create a security for raising capital that corporations will find infinitely alluring, yet one money managers and investors will fall over each other to buy. While fiendishly elusive, the stakes make the game well worth the candle.

A product that fit those requirements came to light in 1985 when the zero-coupon convertible, born out of the fertile mind of Lee Cole of Merrill Lynch, debuted. Over the next six years, before buyers began to realize they had been sold a bill of goods, this one instrument raised over $10 billion for corporations, several hundred million for Merrill, and megamillions for Lee Cole. That may seem like a trivial amount these days, but in the convertible arena, where the total domestic market totals less than $85 billion, $10 billion is big potatoes.

It isn't hard to understand that it took six years before zero-coupon convertibles began to lose their luster, for the "gotcha's" weren't immediately evident, any more than they are in PENs, even in the fine print in the prospectuses. To nose them out, you had to set up a model to consider what might happen under various scenarios. I urged convertible money managers to approach them gingerly, but the issues were snapped up. A large number of buyers, if not the majority, were small retail investors sold by Merrill's far-reaching retail brokerage network.

Of course, putting thumbs down on zeros didn't win any popularity contests at Merrill Lynch, a point of view made absolutely clear when I was pointedly uninvited to attend the roadshow for Disney's European zero-coupon convertible. Just as junk bonds had grown to mammoth proportions a few years earlier, zeros by then had become the biggest game in town. Uninvited didn't mean I was forgotten, however. Word came back: "You may want to date Gina Lolabrigida, but if only Sadie Hawkins is available, date Sadie or you sit home." (Translation: You may want to buy first-quality convertibles, but if only zeros are available, buy zeros or nothing . . . a message fund managers who had bought junk bonds also might have done well to ignore.) Of course, as it turned out, anyone not invited to buy that issue was doubly blessed.

Unlike MCPDPS and PERCS, zero-coupon convertibles are, in fact, convertibles. What makes them so attractive to company treasurers is that no cash interest payments are made. The icing on the cake, moreover, is that the "imputed" interest is deductible as an expense for tax purposes just as if it had actually been paid, so the company not only pays no interest on the capital it borrowed, but it saves taxes, as well.

If that weren't enough, the companies stand to enjoy another savings as well, but one that's not as obvious. Because convertibles can be converted into a fixed number of common shares, investors accept lower interest rates than they'd get on straight bonds or preferreds on the chance that the price of the common will rise lifting the value of the converts. Thus, by issuing convertibles, a company enjoys a break on interest, a break that may later be offset if the price of its stock rises and the convertibles are exchanged for shares at a discount from the existing market price.

In the case of zeros, however, the conversion feature is severely watered down if not virtually worthless. Here's why. A zero-coupon convertible bond is sold at a discount from its value at maturity. A one-year bond with imputed interest of 10%, for example, would be sold for $909. Redeemed a year later for $1,000, investors would then effectively receive the principal plus the interest. Similarly, a 10-year, 10% bond would be sold for $349 and would also be redeemed at maturity for $1,000. As the bond moves closer to maturity (when it will be worth $1,000), its market value rises steadily approaching its value at maturity. After one year, it would have a market value 10% higher, or about $384. At the end of the second year it would be worth about $422, etc.

In the case of a zero that's convertible, however, there's a catch. Since a zero's value rises toward its maturity value, unless the stock rises faster than the imputed interest rate—the rate at which the value of the bond increases— holders receive no benefit from any rise in the stock. Benefits accrue only if a rise in the stock *exceeds* the coupon rate of the bond.

Before putting this subject to rest, it should be noted that although studies compiled in 1990, after the zeros had been in existence for five years, showed that they had substantially underperformed "plain vanilla" convertibles, it wasn't until interest rates plunged in 1991 that real disenchantment set in. It was then that zeros began to renege on another promise, as well.

Perhaps the single most appealing selling feature of zeros was the promise that they'd probably never be called. After all, Merrill Lynch argued, since the yearly tax savings to companies were so attractive, why would they retire them before maturity? On this premise, holders expected that accruing interest would be automatically "reinvested" at the bond's original interest rate throughout the life of the bond—even if interest rates fell—freeing them from scrambling to reinvest cash interest payments at lower interest rates as is necessary with conventional bonds. But when interest rates dropped and one zero after another was called, disillusion set in. The bitterest pill of all, however, may have been when Merrill Lynch itself called a zero it had issued.

PENs

All of which brings us to PENs. With zeros carving out such a hefty share of the convertible market, by the end of the 1980s, other houses were spending late hours struggling to create a hybrid of their own to recapture lost business. MCPDPS and PERCS were two such derivatives masquerading as convertibles. Then, in the summer of 1991, Goldman Sachs unveiled PENs. Standing for Pharmaceutical Exchange Notes, they were billed as a combination zero-coupon convertible and call option. You may wonder how they found buyers for these zero-coupon convertibles for they were sold at par! Buyers paid $1,000 for the bonds with the promise that United Technologies would redeem them for $1,000 in six years. (Perhaps that will catch on: A zero return from a zero coupon.)

Naturally, if that were all, there would have been no buyers. The carrot was the conversion privilege: after one year, these notes could be converted at any time into the cash value of the S&P Pharmaceutical Index if the Index had risen 12.5% or more. (Convertible into 8.25 times the value of the Pharmaceutical Index, which at time of offering was 107.77, the initial conversion value of the bond was $889. Not until the Index rose 12.5% would the conversion value of the bond be worth $1,000.)

Another distinctive feature of these bonds was that while they were issued by and were the obligation of

United Technologies, as part of the deal, United paid Goldman Sachs for the call on the Pharmaceutical Index, so Goldman was on the hook to redeem the call in the same way that any seller of a naked option is obligated to the buyer.

Let's now take PENs apart and see what the buyers really were getting. Zero-coupon convertible bonds sell at a discount from their value at maturity. Since six-year bonds of similar quality to the PENs sold with about an 8.6% coupon at the time, the IRS set the original value of the PENs at $645.60. The balance, $354.40, then represented the amount buyers paid for the call on the Index.

Remember, the exercise price of that call was 12.5% above the current value of the Index. According to the Black-Scholes model, such a call was worth $270, so at $354.40, it was about 30% overpriced. My model (see Chapter 10) suggests it was overpriced by a lot more.

But whether it was fairly priced or not is just part of the question. By presenting these units in a way that persuaded buyers that the full price of the bond would be returned to them after six years, the illusion of safety was created. In fact, the discounted value of $1,000 six years out was only $645.60. Thus buyers were reasonably assured of getting back only a portion of their investment. Worse yet, these units were anything but "safe"!

What buyers surely didn't realize was that they were essentially buying a naked call, but by putting up more than the price of the call, their positions were "deleveraged." For example, if you buy a stock for $100 that goes up 10%, but instead of putting up $100 to buy that stock you put up $200, instead of a 10% return, your return would be only 5%. You halved your risk and halved your return on investment.

Calls on the Pharmaceutical Index had a relative volatility of about 850% (i.e., they were 8.5 times more risky than the average stock). If buyers paid $354.40 for them, they would have been exposed to their full risk. Because they put up $1,000, or about three times the $354.40 value of the calls, their risk was about one-third of 850%, or about 300%, equivalent to three times the risk in the average stock. At three times the risk of the average stock, these bonds were anything but "safe." "Safety" then, was no more than an illusion; it no doubt tempted investors to buy this issue who would not ordinarily consider naked calls.

But not only were these a far more risky investment than many may have realized, the calls were substantially overpriced, as well. Why would sophisticated institutional buyers, buyers who dicker over an eighth of a point, overpay for an instrument of this sort? Was the opportunity to buy a call on the Pharmaceutical Index so tempting, or was it that they didn't really understand what it was they were buying. Evidently, they haven't repealed Lyons' Law: There's a charge for a learning experience.

Spreading Your Wealth

Nifty strategies like spreads, butterflies, straddles, and who knows what else—which in the textbooks offer mouth-watering profits—are inherently difficult to establish at sensible prices and often become even more absurd after the broker carves out his commissions.

Once an investor becomes intrigued with options and sets out to explore the various opportunities they open to him, he soon discovers in all options literature—whether it be basic texts such as *Options as a Strategic Investment* by McMillan, brochures disseminated by the Options Clearing Corporation (OCC), or advanced material like that provided by some brokers—so-called sophisticated spreading strategies that offer the opportunity to make oodles of money.

These strategies go by such intriguing names as spreads (all varieties: bull, bear and neutral, horizontal, vertical and diagonal; not to mention ratio, calendar, and time), butterflies, straddles and trapezoidal hedges, and even . . . strangles. What the literature fails to specify is who these strategies are most likely to make oodles of money for.

THE BULL SPREAD

Let's look at the simplest of the strategies, the bull spread. A bull spread is designed to realize its maximum profit if the underlying stock rises. Thus, the literature counsels, you would want to set up a bull spread on a stock you expect to rise.

Bull spreads may be constructed with calls or puts. If you were constructing one with calls, you'd buy one call and sell another at a higher strike. Both would have the same month of expiration and strike. The immediate advantage is that your outlay is smaller: the premium you take in for the call you sell helps offset the cost of the call you buy.

For example, with a stock at $32, you might set up a spread by buying a call struck at $30 and selling one struck at $35. The call purchased might cost $3 a share and you might receive $1 a share for the other. Your net cost would be $2 a share. Exhibit 7.1 shows the profit/loss profile of this spread as presented in the manuals. Exhibit 7.2 shows what the result would be of simply buying the long call so that we may make a comparison.

Exhibit 7.1   Bull Spread—Stock Price $32

	Strike			Premium			
Buy (Long Call)	$30			$3			
Sell (Short Call)	$35			<u>$1</u>			
Net Cost				$2			

Stock Price at Expiration	**$25**	**$30**	**$32**	**$33**	**$35**	**$40**	**$45**
Long Call at Expiration	$0	$0	$2	$3	$5	$10	$15
Short Call at Expiration	$0	$0	$0	$0	$0	($5)	($10)
Original Cost	<u>($2)</u>	<u>($2)</u>	<u>($2)</u>	<u>($2)</u>	<u>($2)</u>	<u>($2)</u>	<u>($2)</u>
Profit/Loss on Spread	**–$2**	**–$2**	**$0**	**$1**	**$3**	**$3**	**$3**

Exhibit 7.2   Long Call Position Alone

Stock Price at Expiration	**$25**	**$30**	**$32**	**$33**	**$35**	**$40**	**$45**
Long Call at Expiration	$0	$0	$2	$3	$5	$10	$15
Original Call Cost	<u>$3</u>	<u>$3</u>	<u>$3</u>	<u>$3</u>	<u>$3</u>	<u>$3</u>	<u>$3</u>
Profit/Loss on Call	**–$3**	**–$3**	**–$1**	**$0**	**$2**	**$7**	**$12**

According to the manuals, the advantages of the spread are as follows:

1. If the stock doesn't move, which occurs most often, the position breaks even. If you had simply bought the call, you'd lose $1, one-third of your investment.

2. The spread produces a profit on any rise in the stock—not so the call.

3. The spread generates its maximum profit on a very narrow move in the stock. A three-point rise produces a $3-a-share profit. That same rise would produce a profit of only $2 if you had bought the call.

4. If the stock misbehaves, the most you can lose is $2. Had you bought the call, you'd lose $3 or 50% more. The price you pay for this advantage is that you give up the chance to make a whopping profit if the stock takes off, but since you know that really big moves come as rarely as kept promises, you've got yourself sweetly positioned to make small but consistent profits with low risk.

What's Wrong with That Picture?

Like the puzzle pictures, see if you can find four things wrong.

1. Did you spot the first? Favorably priced options aren't lying around like gold nuggets in Sutter's Creek. You have to screen carefully to find one that's overpriced or underpriced. When you con-

struct a position like a spread that combines several different options on the same stock, the task becomes even more formidable, for the options on a stock tend to move together. It's extremely rare to find an underpriced call attractive for buying and an overpriced call attractive for selling on the same stock. To construct an attractively priced spread, then, becomes something of a task.

2. The second is a little more difficult to spot: illustrations such as the one above create the illusion that if the stock rises to $35 or above, you pocket the spread's maximum profit. (Here, that comes to $3 a share.) So pick a stock that's going up and reserve a space in line at the bank! As you'll see, it ain't necessarily so.

3. The third is even less easy to spot, but if you've ever made any investment at all, you didn't do your homework if you didn't spot it. Measuring profits in terms of dollars is misleading; profits must be measured in relation to invested capital.

4. Finally, where are commissions and transaction costs? Few texts, and even fewer brokerage houses or exchange brochures, bother with this aspect of investing. The few that do offer no signposts to warn you exactly where to look for the hidden booby traps. Commissions and transaction costs in trading options can take a significant bite out of potential profits even when a single option is involved. When several options must be bought or

sold to construct a position, the bite can become gluttonous.

The Commission Factor

Exhibit 7.3 shows the bite commissions would take out of the call and spread at a full-cost broker. Notice the extent to which the profit—and the range over which profits are earned—are reduced by commissions.

Exhibit 7.3   After Commissions

Stock Price at Expiration	$25	$30	$32	$35	$40	$45
Spread:						
Original Cost	-2.00	-2.00	-2.00	-2.00	-2.00	-2.00
Value at Expiration	0.00	0.00	2.00	5.00	5.00	5.00
Commissions	0.20	0.20	0.30	0.33	0.50	0.59
Profit/Loss before Commissions	-2.00	-2.00	0.00	3.00	3.00	3.00
Profit/Loss after Commissions	-2.20	-2.20	-0.30	2.67	2.50	2.41
Long Call:						
Original Cost	-3.00	-3.00	-3.00	-3.00	-3.00	-3.00
Value at Expiration	0.00	0.00	2.00	5.00	10.00	15.00
Commissions	0.11	0.11	-0.21	-0.24	-0.28	-0.33
Profit/Loss before Commissions	-3.00	-3.00	-1.00	2.00	7.00	12.00
Profit/Loss after Commissions	-3.11	-3.11	-1.21	1.76	6.72	11.67

Notice the difference between actual profits and the theoretical before-commission profits. Observe the following points:

1. The spread doesn't break even if the stock remains unchanged. Rather, $0.30 a share (15%) would be lost at a full-cost broker or $0.17 a share (8.5%) at a discount broker. That's a far cry from "breaking even."

2. A spread's profit does *not* remain constant as the stock rises. Just as commissions at most brokers are higher for purchasing stock at $40 than at $30, so too do they increase with the price of the option. If the stock was to rise to $45 at expiration, this spread's profits could be as much as 20% below what the manuals would have you believe, depending on where you did business.

3. Commissions take a much bigger bite out of a spread's profits than out of a call's—a serious disadvantage. In contrast to a profit give-up of as much as 20% in a spread, the give-up in a call is just 3%. That's because in a spread there are two option positions to open and there may be two to close at expiration as well, if the stock has risen enough to lift both calls into the money.

   Note: For the purposes of this illustration, commissions are based on rates that would be charged to buy or sell options with a value of $1,000 or more (e.g., 10 or more calls at $1 a share). In-the-money options are closed out at expiration at parity (tangible value); out-of-the-money calls are allowed to expire worthless.

No allowance was made for the possibility that a short option might be exercised. Fewer than 10% of all options are ever exercised, but when they are, commissions are far more expensive. Commissions to buy back 5 calls at $5 amount to about $90; if those calls were exercised, commissions to buy the stock for delivery to the option holder would be about $330, $0.66 a share instead of $0.18 a share.

Institutional investors frequently pay smaller commissions, often $0.05 a share or less. This gives them greater flexibility, but savings are often more than offset by the differential in option premiums that can occur in trading on a large scale. Of course, members of the exchange have almost no transaction costs.

BUTTERFLY SPREAD

If commissions take such an obscene bite out of two-option spreads, imagine what you can expect with strategies that require not two, but three, four, or even more options. The butterfly is one such spread (named, no doubt, for that feeling in your stomach). It's a combination of a bull spread and a bear spread on the same stock. To set it up, two calls are sold at one strike price, one is purchased at a higher strike, and another is purchased at a lower strike. With the stock at $60, for example, you might sell two calls struck at $60, buy one struck at $50, and another struck at $70. Exhibit 7.4 is an example of a butterfly spread that could be created for a net debit of $3 a share. As you can see, before commissions, this position would be profitable at expiration if the stock was between $53 and $67. At $60, the middle strike, it would deliver its maximum profit, $7 a share; at $50 or below, or at $70 or above, the entire original $3 investment would be lost. Exhibit 7.4 illustrates how it looks before commissions begin to nibble away.

Exhibit 7.4   Butterfly Spread—Stock Price $60

	Strike			Premium			
Buy 1 Call	$50			$12			
Buy 1 Call	$70			$3			
Sell 2 Calls	$60			$6			

Stock Price at Expiration	**$50**	**$53**	**$56**	**$60**	**$64**	**$67**	**$70**	**$80**
Long $50 Call at Expiration	$0	$3	$6	$10	$14	$17	$20	$30
Long $70 Call at Expiration	$0	$0	$0	$0	$0	$0	$0	$10
2 Short Calls at Expiration	$0	$0	$0	$0	–$8	–$14	–$20	–$40
Original Debit	–$3	–$3	–$3	–$3	–$3	–$3	–$3	–$3
Profit/Loss								
Before Commission	–3.00	0.00	3.00	7.00	3.00	0.00	–3.00	–3.00
At Discount Broker	–3.31	–0.37	2.61	6.59	2.46	–0.60	–3.64	–3.85
At Full-Cost Broker	**–3.31**	**–0.42**	**2.55**	**6.51**	**2.28**	**–0.83**	**–3.91**	**–4.30**

After commissions, if the stock behaves and stays at $60, the advertised profit of $7 a share shrinks to as little as $6.51. But if the stock rises, the loss soars. At $80 it would be $4.30, 41% higher than the promised maximum. If it rises further, consider moving to Brazil where they don't have extradition.

Should You Spread?

Options are a "pay-to-play" game and the entry fee for spreads is the highest. Think of it like sitting at the tables in Las Vegas with the house cutting the pot every time you call for a card. The more cards you draw (the more options you trade), the more the house takes and the less left for you to win. It is possible, however, to tilt the odds in your favor. To do so, it's necessary to know more about probability, expected returns on investment, and the reward/risk ratio, all of which are discussed in the next chapter. But before moving on, there's a new way to play spreads that you should know about called CAPs.

CAPs

In November 1991, perceiving an opportunity to expand option trading (or perhaps coin a new acronym), the CBOE introduced CAPs. Capped Index Options are vertical spreads (bull spreads and bear spreads) on the S&P 500 Index packaged as a single option. When introduced, a call CAPs was the equivalent of purchasing one at-the-money call (the striking price equivalent to the price of the index) and selling a second call 30 points (about 8%) higher; a put CAPs was the equivalent of buying an at-the-money put and selling a second put 30 points (about 8%) lower. Thus, a bullish position could be established by buying a call CAPs or selling a put CAPs, and a bearish stance could be established by selling a call CAPs or buying a put CAPs.

CAPs offer several advantages to buyers of spreads:

1. Since they trade as a single option, there's commission on only one option instead of two.

2. Because they trade as single options, it's also likely to be easier to place contingent orders with the broker and easier for the floor to execute trades.

3. CAPs are closed out automatically by the exchange at expiration, or as soon as the Index rises to the upper strike of the call CAPs or falls to the lower strike of the put CAPs—the maximum value of either spread. This eliminates the need to monitor the price of the Index and the two individual options, or the need to close out two separate options at fair prices to preserve the indicated profit. (For the writer, however, this is a disadvantage since there is no chance that prices will reverse after a temporary spike in price; but they may find some comfort in the fact that since exercise is not at the discretion of the buyer, it will be easier to predict.)

4. The risk of early exercise of the short option is eliminated.

5. When the spread is closed out, commissions don't escalate with a rise in the Index as they do with a rise in a stock.

But there are disadvantages, too. CAPs are European-style options rather than American. That is, unless exercised by the CBOE when the Index hits the upper or lower strike, they are exercisable only at expiration. That means that there's no opportunity to close out one side of the spread in mid term. Moreover, exercise cannot be retroactive: if the Index crossed the strike that would trigger exercise but, because it was calculated incorrectly, exercise did not occur, there's no recourse. The buyer must hope for the Index to cross the threshold again or wait for expiration. On the other hand, if the Index crossed the strike entirely as a result of miscalculation, exercise takes place; but here, if the error is caught before settlement, exercise is canceled. Sellers should also be aware that exercise occurs if the threshold price is crossed even if trading in other index options is halted. If that happens, sellers may be prevented from taking action to cover their position that they might take in other circumstances.

It is easy to see that CAPs offer better odds to the buyers of spreads, partly because of more favorable transaction costs, partly at the expense of sellers. Considering the way options have proliferated in the past, it is likely that CAPs will eventually spread to other indexes and equity options, as well. Needless to say, because CAPs offer better odds to buyers doesn't guarantee that a specific CAPs will be more attractive for buying or less attractive for selling than a particular spread. Chapter 9, "Probability, Return on Capital and the Reward/Risk Ratio," explores the mechanics, mathematics, and philosophy of how to identify multiple option positions that offer favorable prospects. Before that, however, let's dig into the question of why stock prices rise and fall.

THE LOGICALITY OF ILLOGICAL STOCK PRICES

Why Value Line's Ranking System Works at Times (And When and Why It Doesn't)

Herein we gain an insight into how a system of stock selection that depends primarily on earnings momentum and price can be successful (at times) not by looking into the future but by looking backwards at the past . . . and in doing so, we learn to recognize the forces that drive stocks and the stock market. In this way, we gain an insight into when Value Line's stock selection system is likely to work . . . and when it isn't.

"Yes Virginia, there is hope." With these words Fisher Black, co-creator of the famous Black-Scholes options model and Professor at the Graduate School of Business of the University of Chicago, gave his imprimatur to the Value Line common stock ranking system:

> My position has generally been even more extreme than the strong form of the random walk hypothesis. I have said that attempts to pick stocks that do better than others are not successful. Actively managed portfolios do not do better than buy-and-hold portfolios when transaction and administrative costs are taken into consideration . . . One of the tools for active portfolio management is a ranking system for the performance of stocks. However, just as very few portfolios have been able to pass the test of consistent performance, there are also very few ranking systems that can pass this test. The Value Line ranking system appears to be one of the few exceptions.

Fisher Black delivered this talk at a seminar of the Center for Research in Security Prices in May 1971. It followed extensive tests of the performance of stocks Value Line had recommended since April 1965, when it introduced its unique ranking system. Until then, stocks selected by no other formal system had been demonstrated to consistently outperform the market. (Value Line's ranking system does not forecast that a specific stock will rise or fall; rather it forecasts that the stock will perform better than or worse than the market.)

In its efforts to promote the Investment Survey, which Value Line publishes, Value Line made no secret of how its ranking system worked. In essence, the system, with the exception of one addition, remains basically unchanged to this day. It simply looks for stocks whose earnings are growing faster and whose price/earnings ratio is lower than they have been over the past 10 years relative to other stocks. These two elements, fastest earnings growth and lowest price/earnings ratio, form the primary basis of the system. Some weight is also given to price momentum in recognition of the tendency of a stock whose price has been outperforming other stocks to continues to perform well, and vice versa.

THE THEORY OF INVESTMENT VALUE

While not specifically modeled after J.B. Williams' "Theory of Investment Value," the basis of modern investment theory, Value Line's ranking system captured its essence. The theory holds that the value of a stock is equal to the sum of all future dividends, including the final liquidating dividend, discounted to the present at a rate of interest proportional to the risk or variability of future returns. That says, in effect, that the price/earnings multiple of a stock should be proportional to the rate of earnings growth and inversely proportional to the risk or variability of those earnings.

While the logic of the theory is undeniable, any price for a stock it comes up with is obviously subjective since it depends on estimates of the future dividend stream and the final liquidating dividend. The rate of interest used to discount the future dividend stream is also subjective. Yet though it is unlikely that many realize it, investors intuitively do attempt to get a handle on future dividends in their attempt to forecast profits, for dividends are paid out of profits.

Looking Backwards into the Future

Unfortunately, efforts to forecast future profits suffer from the difficulty of making other than straight-line projections; it is rare, indeed, that an analyst will forecast that a company's earnings will grow 10% next year, 5% the year after that, fall 15% the third year, etc. Rather, forecasts typically assert that earnings are likely to grow by some percentage over the foreseeable future. Worse yet, an examination of published profit forecasts suggests that many are little more than extrapolations of past earnings trends projected into the future. Proof that investors normally value stocks by looking backward rather than into the future is seen in the fact that Value Line's ranking system has worked in many time periods, for the earnings Value Line's rankings depend on are not forecasts of future earnings but profits already reported.

THE RATIONALIZATION FOR IRRATIONAL P/E MULTIPLES

There is another seeming paradox in Value Line's ranking system: though the system's apparent thrust is to search out and recommend stocks with high relative earnings and low relative prices, which is to say, stocks selling at bargain prices relative to their earnings, once recommended, the system will continue to recommend a stock even though its price has soared and the original, attractive price-to-earnings relationship no longer exists. Similarly, once it ranks a stock poorly, indicating that it's likely to underperform the market, it tends to continue to so rank it even after the stock's price has fallen below levels that appear rational.

What is at work here is the relative price momentum factor, which partially overrides other elements of the system. In effect, it is saying that Newton's first law is as applicable in stocks as it is in physics: Bodies in motion tend to remain in motion while bodies at rest tend to remain at rest. This apparent paradox is equally present in Williams' theory of investment value, which also suggests that extraordinarily high or low price/earnings multiples are justified.

Some years ago, I set out to determine if a logical explanation for stratospheric price/earnings multiples could be demonstrated mathematically. What I discovered was that if one is willing to accept analysts' straight-line earnings forecasts and one is also willing to assume that the dividend-to-earnings payout ratio would remain constant, it would not be illogical to expect that the price/earnings multiple would remain constant, too. In other words, if we are willing to assume that earnings growth and the dividend payout ratio will remain constant, then it might be equally appropriate to assume that the price/earnings ratio investors are willing to pay for the stock today will be the same in the future.

On this premise, it can be shown that the price/earnings multiple of a stock should be:

$$P/E = \frac{D\,(1 + G)}{(i - G)}$$

where D = the dividend payout ratio, G = the growth rate of earnings, and i = the rate at which future dividends are discounted to allow for the risk in our growth forecast.

(*Note:* For a further description, see Appendix 8.A.)

Thus, for example, if D = 30%, G = 12% and i = 15%, the appropriate P/E would be:

$$P/E = \frac{.3\,(1+.12)}{(.15-.12)} = \frac{.336}{.03} = 11.2$$

With the help of this simple mathematical relationship, it becomes clear why investors are willing to capitalize high-growth companies so richly. See how the P/E multiple soars as we raise our growth forecast but hold the discount rate constant:

Growth	P/E Multiple
11%	8.3
12	11.2
13	17.0
14	34.2
14.5	68.7
15 or higher	infinite

Notice that as the growth rate (G) approaches the discount rate (i), the denominator (i – G) approaches zero. Of course, when we divide by zero, the result becomes infinite.

Alternately, this simple mathematical relationship makes clear why P/E multiples (and stock prices) soar when interest rates come down. See how the P/E multiple jumps as we lower the discount rate but hold our growth forecast constant:

Discount Rate	P/E Multiple
15%	11.2
14	16.8
13	33.6
13.5	67.2
12	infinite

The fact that a rational explanation can be provided for irrational results does not alter the fact that the results are irrational. Here, of course, these irrational results come about because of the irrational premise that growth will remain constant, and because we assume that we can forecast growth rates with a high degree of accuracy and with modest risk.

Value Line Ranking System's Added Factor

Other than for a single addition, the Value Line common stock ranking system has remained unchanged from its inception. About a dozen years ago, however, another firm published a report showing that Value Line's stock rankings would be enhanced if it adjusted for earnings "surprises," and soon after, Value Line altered its system along lines the study recommended.

Earnings "surprises" are simply profit reports that deviate significantly—10% or more—from expectations. There is little question that other than for broad-scale economic news, which causes all stocks, or those in a homogeneous sector, to heave and ho, the single prime mover of individual stocks is reported earnings. When the earnings figure that hits the tape is much different than expected, it is not unusual for a stock to jump or slump.

FORECASTING THE FORECASTERS

Profit forecasts impact stock prices in two ways: Not only do prices rise and fall with expected profits, but so too does the price/earnings multiple. In the example on page 90, we saw that if, for example, investors expected an annual growth rate of earnings of 13% instead of 12%, all else being the same, the price/earnings multiple could be expected

Exhibit 8.1   How Prices Change with Earnings versus Earnings Growth

	Current Earnings	Perceived Growth Rate	P/E Multiple	Current Price	Forecast Growth	Forecast Earnings	P/E Multiple	Future Price	Percentage Change
(A)	$1.00	12%	11.2	$11.20	12%	$1.12	11.2	$12.54	+12.0%
(A)	$1.00	13%	17.0	$17.00	13%	$1.13	17.0	$19.21	+13.0%
(B)	$1.00	12%	11.2	$11.20	13%	$1.13	17.0	$19.21	+71.5%

to jump from 11.2 to 17.0. To put this in perspective, Exhibit 8.1 illustrates what happens to the price of a stock as earnings grow from year to year and contrasts that to what happens when the forecast rate of earnings growth changes.

As you can see, if the price/earnings multiple remains constant, the change in the price of the stock (and the return to the investor) is equal to the change in earnings ("A"). The really large profits come when the price/earnings multiple rises ("B"). *The most successful investor, then, is not necessarily one who can forecast earnings accurately but one who can forecast what others will forecast and get in early before the price/earnings multiple changes.*

Of course, if you buy a stock with a high price/earnings multiple on the premise that it will go even higher and there's an earnings disappointment, you suffer doubly: not only will the price come down in tandem with earnings, but the price/earnings multiple usually collapses, too.

(*Note:* Whether unusually high price/earnings multiples associated with stocks whose earnings are expected to grow rapidly adequately discount the risk that growth may not live up to expectations would make an interesting study. It is not improbable that high multiples are a product of excessive investor optimism, just as we find in the prices of certain options.)

When to Use and When Not to Use the Value Line Common Stock Ranking System

The abject failure of the Value Line ranking system in the first half of 1992, when the top-ranked stocks substantially underperformed the bottom-ranked stocks, caused investors to really question the efficacy of the company's heralded ranking system for perhaps the first time since Fisher Black published his famous study. In fact, however, since 1982, only the company's singular method of measuring performance perpetuated the myth that the ranking system offered Value Line subscribers a way to beat the market. This is not to say that the system doesn't work at all; it simply doesn't work for Value Line subscribers.

Why Value Line's Published Performance Results Don't Tell the True Story

Whenever you read test results that purport to prove something, it is important to review the questionnaire to be certain that the questions and procedures were directed to the point at issue. Not infrequently, the test may sound as if it proved a point when the questions posed were really irrelevant. Such is the case with the way Value Line measures and reports its performance results.

What Value Line measures and reports is the difference in the appreciation between the stocks it ranked 1 and the stocks it ranked 5. As long as the 1-ranked stocks rose more than the 5-ranked stocks (or fell less), Value Line asserts that the ranking system works, and by investing in the top-ranked stocks, investors would be likely to beat the market. That premise is simply not so. For example, stocks ranked 1 might have risen more than stocks ranked 5 but still underperformed the market.

In addition, Value Line's performance measure excludes dividends. Thus, there is no assurance that even if 1-ranked stocks rose more than 5-ranked stocks (or fell less), that they outperformed them after dividends are included. Value Line's measurements also don't allow for transaction costs, which can be high because of the steady turnover in stock rankings. (Indeed, to contain trading costs, Value Line itself recommends that subscribers buy stocks ranked both 1 and 2 and, once purchased, continue to hold those stocks until their ranks drop to 3.) Thus, the comparison between the performance of 1- and 5-ranked stocks gives no real clue as to how investors who followed Value Line's recommendations really made out. When Value Line's performance results are recalculated on a more objective basis, it turns out that the system only worked during relatively brief periods, and that since 1982 investors who followed the rankings didn't do as well as they would have had they simply bought and held stocks (see Summary at end of this chapter and Exhibits 8.2 and 8.3).

Still, paradoxically, the ranking system does work. It doesn't work all of the time or for all types of stocks or for Value Line subscribers, but it works. The trick is to learn when it works, for which types of stocks, and who it works for, and use the information to improve your own investment returns.

TIMELINESS

One of the reasons that Value Line's ranking system has done so poorly for its subscribers is that others get to use the ranks about 10 days before subscribers. Until a few years ago, Value Line made no secret of the inner workings of its common stock ranking system. Once it became clear that the system could discriminate between the best and worst performing stocks, it was widely copied. Other investors, however, including astute institutional money managers, have a substantial edge in using the system: They can act long before Value Line's ranks reach subscribers. Value Line subscribers must wait for the Value Line Investment Survey to arrive through the mail to learn of rank changes. On average, that's 10 days after the earnings release.[1] Even worse, professional securities analysts and money managers often receive advance warning of an unexpected shift in a company's profit prospects and act accordingly. Except in rare cases, however, Value Line waits until the earnings are actually reported to alter a rank. The result, of course, is predictable: Because so many act in advance of the published ranks, the prices of the issues move well before most Value Line subscribers receive announcement of the rank change. This is one of the single most important reasons why Value Line's ranking system has become increasingly less predictive over the years.

FORECASTING PROFITS

Another reason that Value Line's ranks don't perform as well as they might is inherent in the system itself. Investors may focus myopically on past earnings to forecast future profits, but only if better information isn't available. Not so with the Value Line common stock ranking system. Its focus remains rigidly fixed on the past. Thus, during periods when the investment perspective for the market changes, the ranking system fails miserably.

---

1 Value Line ranks are based on earnings reports that are released through Friday of each week. The rankings then go into the mail timed to reach subscribers the following Friday. Since 1989, the performance of its ranking system has been scored as of the Friday the rankings reach subscribers. Before that, performance was scored the previous Wednesday, or two days earlier than the new rankings reached subscribers. Thus, the ranking system's performance results for the years prior to 1989 may have been overstated.

The system's greatest failure occurs when the outlook for the economy makes a 180-degree turn, from rosy to blah or from blah to rosy. Here's why: In a sour economy, as small, undercapitalized, highly leveraged companies head for the rocks, their earnings sink into red figures, their prices collapse to almost zero, and their (Value Line) ranks sink to 5 (lowest). Let the first hint of an economic recovery peek through the clouds, however, and long before the ranking system responds, bargain hunters swoop in, bidding up these forlorn companies in expectation that disaster will be averted. The huge percentage price gains that follow far outstrip gains of higher-ranked, blue-chip, and growth stocks whose viability was never in doubt.

Just the reverse occurs when a vibrant economy begins to sour. Now, the small, undercapitalized, highly leveraged companies, whose earnings recoveries appeared nothing short of phenomenal, are ranked 1 (highest) just as investors rush off the sinking ship, and prices of these issues plunge while prices of the lower-ranked, more durable blue chips subside only moderately.

For the same reason, the ranking system isn't able to cope with the well-documented "January Effect." In the month or so before January, stocks that performed worst during the year, particularly highly volatile small-cap stocks ranked 5 (lowest), typically get beaten down still further, perhaps by investors looking to take tax losses. Long before the ranks of these stocks turn up, however, bargain hunters swoop in, and their prices rebound vibrantly. But timing this phenomenon is tricky, for the year-end price collapse may begin as early as mid-November or hold off till late December, and the price rebound may begin late or extend into late February, so it is often better to stand clear rather than attempt to play it.

While these system-wide lapses affect broad cross-sections of stocks, the ranking system also fails to predict the performance of individual stocks in various situations. Evidence of a substantial change in a company's prospects—government action, research discoveries, major product innovations or failures, etc.—will precipitate a price movement that the Value Line ranking system, which depends on earnings reports, won't pick up. Money managers who otherwise rely on the ranking system depart from it and act on these announcements, much as they do when earnings reports contradict the ranks.

Other Valuation Measures

The price momentum factor in the common stock ranking system tends to keep stocks with absurdly high price/earnings multiples favorably ranked beyond the point where even the most optimistic investors believe such multiples are justified. Before the ranks change to reflect the change in attitude, investors' allegiance will have switched from "growth" to other criteria of undervaluation, such as the low price-to-book value ratios, low P/E ratios, and so forth. Value Line's ranking system struggles during these well-documented and well-defined periods, for while its price momentum factor will help shift its focus, the primary mechanism of the system remains slavishly tied to earnings growth.

Dividends

The most egregious omission in the Value Line common stock ranking system—and in how it reports its performance—is the absence of dividends. As noted, Value Line's ranks indicate price movement only, not total return, and its performance record ignores dividends, too. While it asserts that dividends would not have a big impact on its results, the argument is not convincing. The absence of dividends not only makes the system appear to discriminate better than it actually does, but it also skews Value Line's recommendations toward growth stocks, which typically pay little or no dividends, and away from better-established stocks, which pay generous dividends. Large, more stable companies that offer sizable dividend yields typically fall through the cracks and are found, by default, among the "average" stocks, those ranked 3. In fact, the yield differential between 1- and 3-ranked stocks over the long term appears to average over 3%, which is often enough to more than offset any appreciation advantage the 1-ranked issues achieve over the market averages.

SUMMARY

The Value Line common stock ranking system has demonstrated an ability to discriminate between stocks that will perform well and those that will perform poorly, but partly because of heavy use of the system by others who are able to act in advance of Value Line subscribers and in part as a result of deficiencies in the system itself, subscribers cannot gain an advantage from using the system as it stands.

Value Line does point out that no one would be able to invest in the way the system's performance is measured (i.e., it would be impossible to buy an equal dollar amount of each of the 100 stocks Value Line ranks highly, nor would an investor be able to realign his portfolio each week to maintain this equal dollar representation), nevertheless, the reporting format still gives an overly optimistic view of the results investors would be likely to achieve. In particular, Value Line directs attention to the "spread" between the performance of the top-ranked and bottom-ranked stocks. For example, if 1-ranked stocks rose 30% and 5-ranked stocks rose 10%, Value Line points to the 20% difference as evidence of the system's ability to discriminate. As an investment tool, this statistic is misleading. An investor measures his performance not in relation to the poorest performing stocks but in relation to the average stock.

In viewing its performance results, bear in mind that no allowance is made for commissions and transaction costs, which can be steep, particularly for the small, thinly traded stocks typically found in the top and bottom ranks. In addition, its failure to account for dividends tends to overstate its discrimination.

But even comparing the performance of the top-ranked stocks to the averages would overstate an investor's probable results, for Value Line advises that stocks ranked both 1 and 2 should be purchased, and the performance of 2-ranked stocks have typically underperformed the 1-ranked stocks. Value Line further advises that once bought, investors should hold stocks until their ranks drop to 3. If an investor managed his portfolio in accordance with this advice, he would likely hold at least three times as many 2-ranked stocks as 1-ranked stocks (the proportion of 2-ranked stocks to 1-ranked stocks is 3-to-1). On that basis, and with allowance for transaction costs and the typical differential in dividend yields between stocks of different ranks, the average annual advantage or disadvantage that could have been gained using Value Line's common stock ranking system is approximately as shown in Exhibit 8.2.

Exhibit 8.2	Advantage of Value Line Common Stock Ranking System versus the Averages*
1965–70	1.8%
1971–75	–1.2%
1976–80	6.1%
1981–85	–0.1%
1986–90	0.1%
1991–92	–2.0%

*These estimates assume an average nine-month holding period, transaction costs of 1% in and out, a ratio of three 2-ranked stocks to each 1-ranked stock held in the portfolio, and a yield disadvantage of just 1.3% for stocks held versus the average stock, equivalent to what it was in the early months of 1992. Note, too, that prior to 1989 the ranking system was scored on prices that existed two days before subscribers received the ranks, so performance of the ranking system for all years before then may have been poorer than shown here.

Thus, if Fisher Black conducted the same test today that he conducted at the end of 1970, it is unlikely he'd again reach the conclusion that the Value Line ranking system offers investors an advantage over a buy-and-hold strategy. Over the last 10 years, an investor who followed Value Line's recommendations would have earned over 6% less than he would by buying and holding stocks selected at random.

Nevertheless, as Exhibits 8.3 and 8.4 illustrate, the common stock ranking system does work during certain periods, particularly when growth stocks are in demand; still, to use it to advantage, an investor must be aware of when the system is likely to discriminate effectively and when it

**Exhibit 8.3   Value Line Ranking System Advantage
versus the Average Stock**

Year	Annual Advantage	Cumulative Compound Advantage
1965	1.064	1.064
1966	0.981	1.044
1967	1.053	1.100
1968	1.001	1.101
1969	1.028	1.131
1970	1.029	1.164
1971	0.984	1.146
1972	0.990	1.135
1973	0.979	1.111
1974	1.010	1.123
1975	0.974	1.094
1976	0.966	1.056
1977	1.064	1.124
1978	1.076	1.210
1979	1.090	1.318
1980	1.114	1.468
1981	0.997	1.463
1982	1.058	1.548
1983	0.921	1.426
1984	0.997	1.421
1985	1.028	1.461
1986	1.019	1.488
1987	1.005	1.496
1988	0.906	1.355
1989	1.044	1.415
1990	1.037	1.467
1991	1.008	1.478
1992	0.979	1.449

Exhibit 8.3 Continued

Assumptions:

1. Ratio of 2-ranked stocks to 1-ranked stocks: 3:1.

2. Transaction costs (in and out): 1%. Turnover: 1.33 times year (average holding period: 9 months).

3. Dividend yield differential between 1- and 2-ranked stocks and the average stock: 1.28% a year (this was the actual spread during the early months of 1992).

---

isn't—and it helps if he can anticipate changes in the rankings, as well.

Further suggestions as to how the system can be used to improve investment performance appear in the "Look to the Future" that appears at the end of the final chapter.

AFTER NOTE

In addition to the common stock ranking system, Value Line has a convertible ranking system and an option ranking system. These systems are substantially different from the common stock ranking system and have been far more successful.

Although both the convertible and option ranking systems use Value Line's common stock ranks as a guide to the probable relative performance of the underlying stock, in other respects they attempt to approximate the way investors actually invest. Issues are evaluated on a total return basis (including dividends and/or interest); recommendations (rankings) are made on a reward/risk basis, relating the projected total return to inherent risk (thus, the number

Exhibit 8.4   Value Line Ranking System
Advantage versus the Average Stock

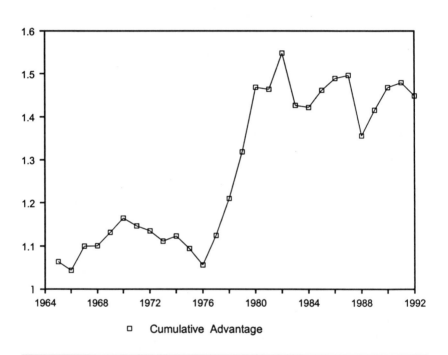

□   Cumulative Advantage

of issues in each rank is not fixed but depends on the re-ward/risk ratio of the issues); relatively illiquid issues whose transaction costs are likely to be high (convertibles that don't trade easily in amounts of $500,000, options with open interest of less than $100,000, and 10-day trading vol-ume of less than $100,000), are ranked, but excluded from the recommendations and the performance results; and the published performance results reflect the performance of both 1- and 2-ranked issues—with allowance for commissions and margin, if applicable.

Both convertible and covered call writing recommendations (both of which are less risky than common stocks) have shown compound average returns of over 20% a year; more risky option strategies have had proportionally higher returns.

APPENDIX 8.A

Derivation of the Price/Earnings Multiple
Where D = Dividend Payout Ratio
        G = Expected Growth Rate of Earnings
        i = Discount Rate
        P = Price/Earnings Multiple
        n = Number of Years

$$PE = \frac{DE(1+G)}{(1+i)} + \frac{DE(1+G)^2}{(1+i)^2} \; \cdots + \; \frac{DE(1+G)^{n-1}}{(1+i)^{n-1}} + \frac{DE(1+G)^n}{(1+i)^n}$$

which simplifies to

$$P = \frac{D(1+G)}{(i-G)}$$

The above formula can't be used if the company pays no dividend, as is often the case for companies expected to achieve a high rate of growth. Instead, the following formula applies:

where P' = future P/E multiple, and
$\quad$ P = present P/E multiple

$$P = \frac{P'(1+G)^n}{(1+i)^n} \quad \text{or} \quad \frac{P'}{P} = \frac{(1+G)^n}{(1+i)^n}$$

Among the anomalies that this formula illustrates is that in the case of a company that pays no dividends, the present P/E multiple is unlimited. It is simply a function of the P/E multiple we are willing to assume will be appropriate in the future.

In addition, when (G), the expected growth rate, is greater than (i), the discount rate, the fraction $(1+G)/(1+i)$ becomes greater than 1 . . . indicating that the present P/E multiple will be greater than the future P/E multiple. But when the growth rate is less than the discount rate, the fraction becomes less than 1, indicating that the present P/E multiple should be less than the future P/E multiple. Finally, if the growth rate is equal to the discount rate, the present P/E multiple will equal the future P/E multiple.

HOW TO EVALUATE OPTIONS

9

Probability, Return on Investment, and the Reward/Risk Ratio

Now that we have seen how commissions can decimate profits, we take another step from the theoretical to the real world by learning how to calculate the profits that are probable rather than merely possible. That leads to return on investment (ROI), a basic of investment analysis frequently overlooked in manuals, and then to our ultimate goal, the reward/risk ratio.

CHAPTER 9

SYNOPSIS

Probability

Probability is the basis of all investing. In the evaluation of options, it plays an essential role in several different ways. The role we examine here is concerned with determining the price the underlying stock is likely to be at some date in the future, usually when the options expire. Probability is simple in concept: it requires no deeper understanding than the realization that if we flip a coin, the probability of heads coming up is 50-50. But though we can predict with reasonable assurance the outcome of a large number of coin tosses, we cannot predict with certainty the outcome of any single toss, or even any series of tosses.

From the discussion of probability here, you will see how predicting the probable future prices of a stock evolves from the toss of a coin. In tossing a coin, however, the probability of heads is equal to the probability of tails. But stock prices cannot decline as much as they can rise (the price of a stock cannot fall below zero), so instead of the "normal" distribution likely when you toss a coin, the number of heads mirrored by the number of tails, stock prices distribute themselves abnormally (or more precisely, "log-normally"), higher prices being more probable than lower prices.

The shape of the log-normal distribution curve, which describes both the range of prices that are likely and the probability of each price occurring, can be determined mathematically. (At the end of this chapter a Lotus-based spreadsheet is described that can be used for this purpose.) With the aid of the log-normal distribution, we can make an informed estimate of the prices at which a stock is likely to be in the future and so the value of an option, or a position combining an option with the stock such as a covered call, or a combination of options such as a spread.

Return on Invested Capital

Return on invested capital, or more simply return on investment (ROI), is a fundamental of all investing, yet one frequently ignored by professionals as well as neophytes. That an investment offers a $2,000 profit means almost nothing unless we know how much capital must be committed and the period of time we must wait in order to earn that sum. A convenient way to compare investments then is in terms of the annualized return. Although to compare investments in this way makes the assumption, not always warranted, that after the original investment is closed out, a similar rate of return can be earned on the reinvested capital throughout the balance of the year, nevertheless it provides a starting point for comparing one investment against another.

The Reward/Risk Ratio

The reward/risk ratio is the final step in the evaluation of any investment. An expected annualized return on investment of 25% is attractive for most stocks but not for naked options where the risk of loss is high.

Risk, of course, is simply a measure of price volatility. An investment that we know can always be cashed out at full face value, like an insured bank account, has zero risk. Virtually all other investments, even government bonds and T-bills, have some degree of risk.

If we consider risk in terms of the average stock, it becomes more easy to visualize. For example, a stock 25% more volatile than the average stock would be said to have a "relative volatility" of 125%, and one 60% as volatile as the average stock would be said to have a relative volatility of 60%.

This makes it simple to describe risk in other instruments, as well. For an option, we can measure how much faster its price is likely to move than its underlying stock. If it moved six times faster than its underlying stock and the stock's relative volatility was 120%, the relative volatility of the option would be 720%.

"Relative volatility" also makes it easy to identify what might be an appropriate reward/risk ratio. Historically, the average stock has provided an average return of about 12% a year. That gives it a reward/risk ratio of 0.12 (12%/100%). To be adequately compensated for risk, then, we would expect a similar reward/risk ratio from other investments. For an option with a relative volatility of 500% to have a reward/risk ratio of 0.12, it would have to promise a return of 60% (500% × 0.12). On the other hand, a return of 9% would be sufficient for a less-risky investment with a relative volatility of 75% (75% × 0.12).

PROBABILITY

In Chapter 7, we examined the profit/loss profiles of two different spreads. Exhibit 9.1 reproduces the profile of the bull spread.

Notice that we can't tell whether it would be advantageous to buy this spread, sell it, or do neither. To make this decision, we need to know the probable prices the stock is

Exhibit 9.1   Bull Spread—Stock Price $32

	Strike			Premium		
Buy (Long Call)	$30			$3		
Sell (Short Call)	$35			$1		
Net Cost				$2		

Stock Price at Expiration	$25	$30	$32	$35	$40	$45
Long Call at Expiration	$0	$0	$2	$5	$10	$15
Short Call at Expiration	$0	$0	$0	$0	–$5	–$10
Original Cost	–$2	–$2	–$2	–$2	–$2	–$2

Profit/Loss on Spread

Before Commissions	–$2.00	–$2.00	$0.00	$3.00	$3.00	$3.00
At Discount Broker	–2.11	–2.11	–0.17	2.82	2.72	2.67
At Full-Cost Broker	–2.20	–2.20	–0.30	2.67	2.50	2.41

likely to be at when the options expire, what return on investment we'd earn if the stock is at such prices, how much risk we take in establishing this spread, and whether the potential return is adequate compensation for the risk.

Earlier, I mentioned that a high level of mathematics was not necessary to understand and trade options but that an understanding of probability is a great help. Probability is a measure of the likelihood of an event occurring. One securities analyst noted that 90% of his forecasts were within 2% of actual 10% of the time. That, too, is probability (though if he wasn't joking, he should find another line of work).

Probability is simple to understand and calculate, though the calculations can become a bit of a chore. Fortunately, these calculations can be done for you with the aid of simple computer programs, such as the one you'll find at the end of this chapter. It is advantageous, however, to understand the concept of probability.

Probability tells us that the toss of a coin gives us a 50-50 chance of a head turning up. If we toss the coin a second time, we have a 25% chance that heads will come up twice in a row, a 25% chance of two tails, and a 50% chance of one head and one tail. If we take one toss at a time, it becomes simple to follow:

Toss 1: There are just two possibilities, both of which are equal, a head or a tail, thus we have:

                      HEAD   TAIL

Toss 2: Again, there are just two possibilities, both of which are equal, a head or a tail. Thus, when we combine it with toss one, we have:

Result of:

Toss 1:   HEAD   TAIL
                      / \\   / \\
Toss 2:   HEAD   TAIL   HEAD   TAIL
               | | | |
Result: HEAD-HEAD HEAD-TAIL   TAIL-HEAD TAIL-TAIL

Of the four possible combinations, two heads comes up once (25% probability), two tails comes up once (25%), and a head and a tail come up twice (50%).

Let's take this one step further. The first time we tossed we had two possible outcomes. The second time, four. If we toss the coin a third time, we will have eight possible outcomes, as follows:

Result of Toss 2:

HEAD-HEAD	HEAD-TAIL	TAIL-HEAD	TAIL-TAIL
/ \	/ \	/ \	/ \

Toss 3:

HEAD	TAIL	HEAD	TAIL	HEAD	TAIL	HEAD	TAIL
I	I	I	I	I	I	I	I

Result:

H-H-H	H-H-T	H-H-T	H-T-T	H-H-T	H-T-T	H-T-T	T-T-T

Of the eight possible outcomes, we have the following:

Outcome	Frequency	Probability
3 Heads	1	1 of 8, or 12.5%
2 Heads/1 Tail	3	3 of 8, or 37.5%
2 Tails/1 Head	3	3 of 8, or 37.5%
3 Tails	1	1 of 8, or 12.5%
Totals:	8	100.0%

All probability is just this simple. The outcomes of each event (toss) are simply combined with the outcomes of each subsequent event (toss). Of course, the odds of an event occurring need not be 50%. Our "coin" could have been weighted so that the odds of a head were 60% and the odds of a tail 40%, in which case, out of 10 tosses, we would expect 6 tails and 4 heads, as follows:

H H H H H T T T T T

If we toss that coin, we can determine the odds of various outcomes with a diagram, as we did above (or we can simply multiply the probability of each outcome by the probability of subsequent outcomes).

First toss:	60% HEADS		40% TAILS

First toss: 60% HEADS   40% TAILS

                / \   / . \

Second toss: 60% HEAD S 40% TAILS   6 0% HEADS 40% TAILS

                | | | |

Result:

    2 HEADS = 36% HEAD-TAIL = 24%   HEAD-TAIL = 24% 2 TAILS = 16%

So the probable outcomes are:

2 HEADS	36%
1 HEAD-1 TAIL	48%
2 TAILS	16%
Total:	100%

Needless to say, our "toss" might have more than two outcomes. If we rolled one die of a pair of dice, any of six numbers could come up, each with equal probability. If the dice were loaded, however, the probability of each number coming up would not be equal.

We can also calculate probability easily if we combine different events. What, for example, is the probability of rolling the number 4 with one dice and flipping a coin and having a head come up? Here, we have 1 chance in 6 of the number 4 coming up and 1 chance in 2 of a head coming up, so in total, we have 1 chance in 12.

Let's now apply probability to option trading.

PROBABILITY AND STOCK PRICE DISTRIBUTION

Probability shows that random events distribute themselves in the pattern of the familiar bell-shaped curve. (See Exhibit 9.2.) The width of the curve describes the range of the distribution; the height describes the probability of occur-

Exhibit 9.2   Normal Distribution

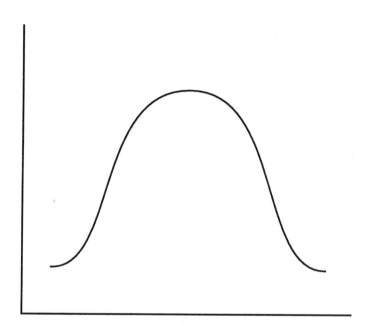

rence. If we were drawing a distribution curve of the probable outcome of tossing a coin twice, it would look like this:

50%		H-T	
25%	H-H		T-T

Notice that heads-tails is likely to come up 50% of the time and so it commands the highest point in the distribution "curve"; two heads or two tails are likely to come up only 25% of the time, so they are half the height and further removed from the central event.

If we were drawing a distribution curve of the outcome of tossing a coin four times, it would look like this:

37.50%		H-H-T-T	
25.00%		H-H-H-T	T-T-T-H
6.25%	H-H-H-H		T-T-T-T

What we see is that as we increase the number of tosses, the number of possible combinations increases so the curve becomes wider; at the same time, the probability of the central event occurring becomes smaller, so the curve becomes flatter. The bell-shaped curve then describes a "normal" distribution.

NORMAL VERSUS LOG-NORMAL DISTRIBUTION

As you can see, the bell-shaped curve describes perfect symmetry. The probability of an event occurring on one side is identical to the probability of the opposite event occurring. Stock prices do not distribute themselves quite so symmetrically, however. This is so, in part, because there is a lower limit to which the price of a stock may drop (zero). A stock initially at $20 can rise 40 points to $60 but it can fall only 20 points. The result is that the shape of the curve is skewed to the right. Rather than a "normal" distribution, stock prices become distributed in the pattern of a "log-normal" distribution. (See Exhibit 9.3.)

The height and width of log-normal curves are determined not unlike the height and width of the bell-shaped probability curves. In the bell-shaped probability curves, we saw that the number of times we tossed the coin, the broader the curve became. Similarly, the relationship of

Exhibit 9.3   Log-Normal Distribution

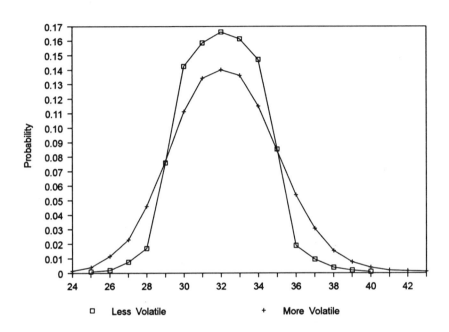

width to height in the log-normal curve depends on the length of time that prices are allowed to distribute and (as you would expect) the volatility of the stock's price movement. The greater the length of time or the more volatile the stock, the broader the price range; conversely, the shorter the time period or the more stable the stock, the narrower the range over which prices are likely to be distributed.

How a stock's prices are likely to distribute can be determined by means of a mathematical formula for log-normal distribution. Only three items of information are required: the initial price of the stock, its volatility, and the length of time over which prices may fluctuate. The formulas for this curve can be found in most texts. A simple Lotus-based spreadsheet incorporating the formula, which shows the range of prices and the probability of each price actually occurring, appears at the end of this chapter. We have used this spreadsheet to evaluate the bull spread that we discussed at the beginning of this chapter. (See Exhibit 9.4.)

EXPECTED VALUE

Column C of Exhibit 9.4 shows the probability of this stock being at prices shown in Column A when the options expire. The stock, initially, was $32. Notice that is the most likely price for this stock in the future. The probability of the stock being $32 is 14.0%. The probability that it will be at higher prices or lower prices declines as the price moves away from $32.

These probabilities are of use to us in calculating the likely value of an option on this spread. Think of it as calculating the probability of earning a profit flipping a weighted coin. If a coin was weighted so that there was a 60% probability of heads and 40% probability of tails, you'd bet on heads, of course. But would you bet on heads if you'd win $5 if heads came up but would lose $7 if tails came up? Yes, certainly. You'd have a 60% chance of winning $5, so weighing the probability of heads you determine that you would be likely to win $3 (60% × $5) against a probability of losing $2.80 (40% × $7). Adding the two

**Exhibit 9.4   Probable Profit (or Loss) from Spread
(Before Commissions)**

A	B	C	D
	Value of Bull Spread at This Price	**Probability of Stock Being between This and Next Lower Price**	**Weighted Value**
Stock	**(1)**	**(2)**	**(1) x (2)**
$24	($2)	0.2%	($0.003)
$25	($2)	0.4%	($0.008)
$26	($2)	1.2%	($0.023)
$27	($2)	2.3%	($0.046)
$28	($2)	4.6%	($0.092)
$29	($2)	7.7%	($0.153)
$30	($2)	11.1%	($0.223)
$31	($1)	13.4%	($0.134)
$32	$0	14.0%	$0.000
$33	$1	13.6%	$0.136
$34	$2	11.5%	$0.230
$35	$3	8.4%	$0.253
$36	$3	5.4%	$0.161
$37	$3	3.1%	$0.092
$38	$3	1.5%	$0.046
$39	$3	0.8%	$0.023
$40	$3	0.4%	$0.012
$41	$3	0.2%	$0.006
$42	$3	0.2%	$0.005
$43	$3	0.1%	$0.003
Totals		100.0%	$0.285

Note: The increment between prices in Column 1 can be set at whatever interval desired. The smaller the increment, the more precise the profit estimate. Note also that Column 3 shows the probability of the price being between the price shown on that line and the line above. Probabilities (%) shown here are approximate, for illustration only.

together, you find that in the long run, you'd be likely to win $0.20 each time the coin was flipped.

All probable return is figured the same way, by multiplying the probability of each event by the gain or loss earned if that event occurred, then totaling the results of the products. Column B of Exhibit 9.4 shows the profit or loss earned by the bull spread at each stock price, Column C the probability that that price will occur, and Column D the "weighted" profit or loss at each price. When the products in Column D are added together, we find that the spread is likely to yield a profit of $0.285 a share.

That's before commissions, of course. In the real world, values in Column B must be adjusted to allow for commissions, as we have done in Exhibit 9.5. Notice that if we were trading through a discount broker, the expected profit shrinks from $0.285 to $0.123 a share; at a full-cost broker, instead of a profit, we'd be likely to suffer a loss of $0.01 a share.

Clearly, we wouldn't set up this spread at a full-cost broker. But would we at a discount broker, or if we didn't pay commissions? We can only answer that question if we compare the indicated return on investment to the risk.

RETURN ON INVESTMENT

Even so-called experts forget the proper measure of investment returns. In the fall of 1991, Salomon Brothers was found to have been illegally cornering the government's Treasury note auctions. The firm was in jeopardy of following Drexel Burnham to the junkyard (Drexel had gone defunct not long before, following the discovery that Michael

Exhibit 9.5   Expected Profit from Bull Spread Before and After Commissions

Stock ($)	Proba- bility	Value Before Com- mission ($)	Probable Value ($)	At Discount Broker ($)	Probable Value ($)	At Full- Cost Broker ($)	Probable Value ($)
24	0.2%	−2.00	−0.003	−2.11	−0.003	−2.20	−0.003
25	0.4%	−2.00	−0.008	−2.11	−0.008	−2.20	−0.008
26	1.2%	−2.00	−0.023	−2.11	−0.024	−2.20	−0.025
27	2.3%	−2.00	−0.046	−2.11	−0.049	−2.20	−0.051
28	4.6%	−2.00	−0.092	−2.11	−0.097	−2.20	−0.101
29	7.7%	−2.00	−0.153	−2.11	−0.162	−2.20	−0.169
30	11.1%	−2.00	−0.223	−2.11	−0.235	−2.20	−0.245
31	13.4%	−1.00	−0.134	−1.16	−0.156	−1.29	−0.173
32	14.0%	0.00	0.000	−0.17	−0.023	−0.30	−0.043
33	13.6%	1.00	0.136	0.83	0.113	0.69	0.094
34	11.5%	2.00	0.230	1.82	0.210	1.68	0.193
35	8.4%	3.00	0.253	2.82	0.238	2.67	0.226
36	5.4%	3.00	0.161	2.76	0.149	2.57	0.138
37	3.1%	3.00	0.092	2.75	0.084	2.55	0.078
38	1.5%	3.00	0.046	2.74	0.042	2.53	0.039
39	0.8%	3.00	0.023	2.73	0.021	2.51	0.019
40	0.4%	3.00	0.012	2.72	0.010	2.50	0.010
41	0.2%	3.00	0.006	2.72	0.005	2.49	0.005
42	0.2%	3.00	0.005	2.71	0.004	2.48	0.004
43	0.1%	3.00	0.003	2.71	0.003	2.47	0.003
Totals	100.0%		$0.285		$0.123		−$0.010

Note: Probabilities (%) shown here are approximate, for illustration only.

Milken had been dealing off the bottom of the deck in junk bonds). Acting quickly to avert that fate, Salomon swept its chairman out the door, replaced him with Warren Buffet, a large shareholder, and launched a massive public relations drive to persuade American and foreign regulators and investors that with the change in management, Mr. Scrungy had become Mr. Clean. As the team got up to the line of scrimmage, Salomon's salesmen were dispatched hither and yon to wine, and dine customers, beginning with those who had turned coolest. And so I soon found myself being lavishly dined at Le Cirque, one of the favorite New York restaurants, double-teamed by two members of the Salomon staff. As is the way of these $700 evenings-for-three (limousines included, so that the splendor of the evening is not undone by a grungy subway ride home), the talk ultimately segued from good fellowship and the latest football scores to the real purpose of the evening.

"Are we in the penalty box?" one of the staff members asked me. "After all," he offered, "there's a lot of fuss, but it wasn't as if Salomon made any huge amount of money out of this. Salomon had $100 million committed to the government's Treasury note auction and earned only one million or two."

(An image of the closing courtroom argument popped irreverently into my mind: "Gee, judge, my client spent $100 to buy that gun and got only $2 in the holdup. What's all the fuss?") Irreverence aside, a King Solomon this Salomon wasn't. What my host failed to point out was that Salomon "earned" that $2 million in just one day. That's equivalent to a return on capital of over 1,000% a year!

How much of a return would the bull spread we have been discussing provide? We saw that at a discount broker a buyer of this spread stood to earn a profit of $0.123 after commissions on an outlay of $2.11, indicating a return of 5.8% ($0.123/$2.11).[1] A return like that wouldn't tempt us if it would be earned over a year. But if the options expire in 45 days, it's the equivalent of an annual return of 57%.[2]

Exhibit 9.6   Annualized Return on Investment

Where: T = time in days
          R = return on investment (in percentage)

then:

$$\text{Annualized Return} = (1 + R)^{\frac{360}{T}} - 1$$

or . . .

$$= (1.058)^{\frac{360}{45}} - 1$$

$$= 57.3\%$$

---

1 The buyer of a spread lays out no more than the original debit incurred in setting up the spread as long as profits from the long option will cover any losses on the short option. (This will occur whenever the long option expires no earlier than the short option and, if constructed with calls, the long call has the lower strike or, if constructed with puts, the long put has the higher strike.) A seller of a spread must post margin equal to the maximum loss to which he is exposed, or the difference between the two strikes. The credit received on sale of the spread may be applied against the margin requirement. A seller of this spread, for example, would post margin of $5, the difference between the strikes. The $2 credit could be applied against that making the net outlay about $3. Buyers and sellers, in addition, must pay out commissions at the time the spread is established.

2 Exhibit 9.6 contains a formula for calculating annualized returns on investments.

RISK, VOLATILITY, AND RELATIVE VOLATILITY

In investing, return and risk go hand in hand. An annualized return of 57% sounds attractive, but if the risk is 20 times greater than the average stock's, would it really be? Ultimately, then, returns must be related to risk.

As described, one of the more convenient ways to conceptualize risk is relative to the average stock. If we assign the average stock a "relative volatility" of 100%, the risk in other investments can be easily compared. A stock 25% more volatile than the average stock, for example, would have a relative volatility of 125%; another stock, 60% as volatile as the average stock, would have a relative volatility of 60%.

To measure the relative volatility of an option is a simple matter: we multiply the relative volatility of the underlying stock by the leverage of the option. (Leverage measures how much faster the option's value changes than the stock's.) If an option's value changes 10 times as fast as the stock's, its relative volatility would be 10 times the stock's. Similarly, the risk or relative volatility of a spread is simply the relative volatility of the underlying stock multiplied by the leverage of the spread.

Exhibit 9.7 illustrates how to calculate the relative volatility of an option position such as our bull spread. (For an explanation of the calculations, see bottom of Exhibit 9.7.) Here, we found that the spread's leverage is 11.1 times that of the stock. It is 11.1 times as volatile, or 11.1 times as risky. Thus, if the stock has a relative volatility of 100%, the spread would have a relative volatility of 1,110%.

Exhibit 9.7   Calculating Leverage and Relative Volatiltity

A	B	C	D	E	F	G	H
Stock	Value of Spread	Proba-bility of Stock Being at This Price	Weighted Value B × C	Percentage Change in Value of Stock	Spread	Leverage F/E	Weighted Leverage G × C
$24	($2.11)	0.2%	($0.00)	−25%	−100%	4.0	0.01
$25	($2.11)	0.4%	($0.01)	−22%	−100%	4.6	0.02
$26	($2.11)	1.2%	($0.03)	−19%	−100%	5.3	0.06
$27	($2.11)	2.3%	($0.05)	−16%	−100%	6.4	0.15
$28	($2.11)	4.6%	($0.10)	−13%	−100%	8.0	0.37
$29	($2.11)	7.7%	($0.16)	−9%	−100%	10.7	0.82
$30	($2.11)	11.1%	($0.23)	−6%	−100%	16.0	1.78
$31	($1.16)	13.4%	($0.16)	−3%	−55%	17.6	2.36
$32	($0.17)	14.0%	($0.02)	0%	−8%		
$33	$0.83	13.6%	$0.11	3%	39%	12.6	1.71
$34	$1.82	11.5%	$0.21	6%	86%	13.8	1.59
$35	$2.82	8.4%	$0.24	9%	134%	14.3	1.20
$36	$2.76	5.4%	$0.15	13%	131%	10.5	0.57
$37	$2.75	3.1%	$0.09	16%	130%	8.3	0.26
$38	$2.74	1.5%	$0.04	19%	130%	6.9	0.10
$39	$2.73	0.8%	$0.02	22%	129%	5.9	0.05
$40	$2.72	0.4%	$0.01	25%	129%	5.2	0.02
$41	$2.72	0.2%	$0.01	28%	129%	4.6	0.01
$42	$2.71	0.2%	$0.01	31%	128%	4.1	0.01
$43	$2.71	0.1%	$0.00	34%	128%	3.7	0.00
		100%	$0.12				11.1

Note: The weighted average leverage of a position is determined by calculating the leverage at each price (Column G) and multiplying that leverage by the probability of that price (Column H). The sum of the weighted leverage figures in Column H is the weighted average leverage of the position. Here, the weighted average leverage is 11.1. Probabilities (%) shown here are approximate, for illustration only.

CHAPTER 9

THE REWARD/RISK RATIO

What return should we demand from an option position with a relative volatility of 1,110%? Earlier, we found that the expected annualized return on investment for the spread was 57.3%. Is this sufficient?

The average stock offers a return of approximately 12% a year. Thus, if we are to take 11.1 times the risk, to get a return that adequately compensates us for the additional risk, we would want an annualized return 11.1 times as great. That amounts to 133% (11.1 × 12%). Only if this spread promised an annualized return of 133% or more would it make sense.

We express this in terms of a reward/risk ratio. The average stock has a reward/risk ratio of 0.12 (12%/100%). Assuming we were willing to take a position that had 11.1 times as much risk, we'd do so only if its indicated reward/risk ratio was 0.12 or greater. This spread has a reward/risk ratio of only 0.05 (57.3%/1,110%). It is clearly unsuitable.

Would this spread make sense under other conditions? Certainly. If we paid no commissions, the spread would offer an annualized return of 190%, in which case it would boast a reward/risk ratio of 0.17.[3]

---

[3] If no commissions were involved, the leverage of the spread would change very slightly, as well, but the reward/risk ratio would still be well within the desired range.

SUMMING UP

To be sure the odds are in your favor take the following steps:

1. Calculate the expected value of the option position after commissions making use of the log-normal price distribution to estimate the probable prices of the underlying stock at expiration and the probability of each price.

2. Estimate the annualized return on investment by dividing the expected value of the position by the investment.

3. Calculate the leverage of the option position and determine its risk by multiplying the leverage by the relative volatility of the underlying stock.

4. If the relative volatility of the position is within the range acceptable to you and the reward/risk ratio is 0.12 or greater, you can consider opening the position. But be careful: If you accept a smaller reward/risk ratio, you are taking unfavorable odds. Investments that stick you with short odds will pay off occasionally, and sometimes pay off handsomely, just like the slots in Las Vegas. Over time, however, taking the short odds guarantees to shave your returns or, worse yet, put you in a hole. If the expected reward/risk ratio of an investment is not as

good as that of the average stock, forget it. You'd be better off buying stocks.

5. Don't make the assumption that just because the reward/risk ratio is favorable you're assured of success. After all, if you're going after a 10-to-1 payoff, even if you tilt the odds in your favor, the odds of success aren't likely to be too much better than 1-in-10. To reduce the chance of loss, it's necessary to diversify away your risk, a topic discussed in a later chapter.

APPENDIX 9.A
Probability Distribution as It Looks in a Lotus Spreadsheet

	A	B	C	D	E	F	G
1			LOG-NORMAL DISTRIBUTION				
2			(*Probability stock will be between this				
3			price and next lower price.)				
4			——————————————				
5	$30.000	–Initial Price					
6	35.000%	–Volatility				PRICE	
7	60	–# Days				DISTRIBUTION	
8	Prices	Calculations				Cumulative Discrete*	
9		===================					
10	14.00	–5.4	0	0	0	0.0%	0.0%
11	15.00	–4.9	0	0	0	0.0%	0.0%
12	16.00	–4.4	0	0	0	0.0%	0.0%
13	17.00	–4.0	0	1	0	0.0%	0.0%
14	18.00	–3.6	0	1	0	0.0%	0.0%
15	19.00	–3.2	0	1	0	0.1%	0.0%

APPENDIX 9.A Continued

	A	B	C	D	E	F	G
16	20.00	-2.9	0	1	0	0.2%	0.1%
17	21.00	-2.5	0	1	0	0.6%	0.4%
18	22.00	-2.2	0	1	0	1.4%	0.8%
19	23.00	-1.9	0	1	0	3.1%	1.6%
20	24.00	-1.6	0	1	0	5.8%	2.7%
21	25.00	-1.3	0	1	0	10.0%	4.2%
22	26.00	-1.0	0	1	0	15.7%	5.7%
23	27.00	-0.7	0	1	0	22.9%	7.2%
24	28.00	-0.5	0	1	0	31.4%	8.5%
25	29.00	-0.2	0	1	0	40.6%	9.2%
26	30.00	-.0	0	1	0	50.0%	9.4%
27	31.00	0.2	0	1	0	59.1%	9.1%
28	32.00	0.5	0	1	0	67.5%	8.4%
29	33.00	0.7	0	1	0	74.9%	7.4%
30	34.00	0.9	0	1	0	81.1%	6.2%
31	35.00	1.1	0	1	0	86.1%	5.0%
32	36.00	1.3	0	1	0	90.0%	3.9%
33	37.00	1.5	0	1	0	93.0%	3.0%
34	38.00	1.7	0	1	0	95.2%	2.2%
35	39.00	1.8	0	1	0	96.8%	1.6%
36	40.00	2.0	0	1	0	97.9%	1.1%
37	41.00	2.2	0	1	0	98.6%	0.7%
38	42.00	2.4	0	1	0	99.1%	0.5%
39	43.00	2.5	0	1	0	99.4%	0.3%
40	44.00	2.7	0	1	0	99.7%	0.2%
41	45.00	2.9	0	1	0	99.8%	0.1%
42	46.00	3.0	0	1	0	99.9%	0.1%
43	47.00	3.2	0	1	0	99.9%	0.1%
44	48.00	3.3	0	1	0	100.0%	0.0%
45	49.00	3.5	0	1	0	100.0%	0.0%
46	50.00	3.6	0	1	0	100.0%	0.0%

Cell Formulas for Lotus Spreadsheet on Page 132.

CHAPTER 9

Cell Formulas for Lotus Spreadsheet

A5:	–Initial Price	(Enter stock's initial price)
A6:	–Volatility	(Enter stock's annual volatility)/100
A7:	–# Days	(Enter number days position to be held)

Cell Formulas

A10..A79:	Insert prices over desired price range
B10:	@LN(A10/$A$5)/($A$6*@SQRT($A$7/365))
C10:	0.3989423*(@EXP(–0.5*B10*B10))
D10:	(1/(1+0.2316419*@ABS(B10)))
E10:	1–(1.330274*D10^5–1.821256*D10^4+1.781478*D10^3–
	0.356538*D10^2+0.3193815*D10)*C10
F10:	@IF(B10>0,1–E10,E10)
G10:	+F10–F9

Copy Cell Formulas in B10..G10 to B79..G79 (or as far down as you'd like).

Note: As discussed in Chapter 3, "Implied Future Volatility," price distribution is based on a forecast of the stock's future volatility.

Pricing Options

Heresy! As we explore how options are priced, we discover that we have been gulled! The buyer and the seller of an option DO NOT have positions opposite to each other! That being so, then we must conclude that Black-Scholes, Cox-Ross-Rubenstein, and other models that the industry has accepted as gospel really don't price options correctly! Further, we also discover that risk is NEGATIVE price movement, and that argues that the standard method of determining investment risk—by measuring TOTAL price movement—also isn't likely to price options correctly!

VALUING AN OPTION

Until now, I have discussed options on the basis that the buyer's position is exactly opposite to the seller's, a conception that appears fairly universal. While it is true that if commissions are ignored, whatever profit or loss the buyer realizes is exactly equal to the profit or loss suffered by the seller, paradoxically the two positions are not mirror images of each other at all. If this can be demonstrated to be so, then mathematical models—which assume there is a single value for an option that equates the buyer's and the seller's positions, such as the Black-Scholes model and others, obviously cannot be correct.

The fact that the positions of the buyer and the seller are not mirror images of each other can be demonstrated rather easily. Assume, for example, that an option is expected to have a value of $5 at expiration. A buyer of that option, then, must pay less than $5 simply to break even— that is, earn a return on his capital. (Indeed, all option models assert that an allowance is made for a fair return on capital.) The seller, on the other hand, who will have to buy back the option for $5, has a cash investment too: he must post margin to cover his short position. Consequently, simply to break even—that is, earn as much as he could otherwise on his capital—he must sell the option for more than $5. Obviously, if the buyer must pay less than $5 to break even and the seller must sell it for more than $5 to break even, there cannot be a single value for the option that is "fair" for both the buyer and the seller, as option models assert.

(*Note:* If the seller of the option received the cash up front and had no margin requirement, the argument that the buyer's position and the seller's position are the mirror images of each other would be supportable. But this, of course, is not the case. Both must put money up front, and so both are entitled to earn a return on capital.)

Since we cannot set a single value on an option that's fair for both the buyer and the seller, it's clear that the appropriate value of an option depends on whether we plan to buy it or sell it.

SYNOPSIS

Based on the remarks above and the discussions in previous chapters, there should be no mystery about how an option should be valued from the perspective of the buyer, seller, or covered writer. The following three things must be known:

1. *The probable value of the position at expiration.* The probable value of the option at expiration depends, of course, on the probable value of the underlying stock at expiration, which we can determine with the help of the log-normal distribution formula.

2. *Risk.* The traditional way to measure a stock's risk is in terms of price volatility. The traditional way to measure an option's risk is by comparing how fast its price moves relative to the stock's. For example, if the option's price changes by 80% on a 10% change in the stock, the option's "leverage" is eight times. It moves eight times faster than the stock, so

it is eight times as risky. If the stock's relative volatility was 100%, then the option's relative volatility would be 800%. Price movement in the option relative to the stock can be compared most easily at expiration, when the option will trade at its tangible value.

The traditional method of measuring risk in terms of volatility comes into question, however, when we consider that volatility is measured in terms of total price movement, both favorable and unfavorable. But is favorable price movement "risk"? For most investors, obviously not. "Risk," to them, is the risk of loss, not the "risk" of profit. If the risk of loss was always proportional to the total risk, either would prove equally useful in valuing options. This is not the case, however. Certain options can be valued correctly only on the basis of the risk of loss.

Though log-normal stock price distribution indicates that the likelihood of higher prices is greater than the likelihood of lower prices, when the percentage change is measured in terms of logs, higher and lower prices are equally likely. This can be understood more easily if we look at a stock whose price has risen and consider the percentage that price must fall to return to its original price. Consider, for example, a stock that rose from $10 to $25 or another which fell from $10 to $4. In log terms, both movements are equal: at $25, the stock must fall 60% to return to $10, the same percentage that the stock moved falling from $10 to $4. Expressed in logs, the percentage rise from $10 to $25 or fall from $10 to $4 is an identical 91.63%.

It is on this log basis, then, that statisticians assert that the likelihood of higher and lower prices are equal. This defines risk from the perspective of log-normal price movement, but it doesn't apply to the risk an investor faces. If an investor buys two stocks at $10 and one rose to $25 while the other fell to $4, he'd have a $15 profit on one and a $6 loss on the other for a net gain of $9—hardly a break-even situation. In trading options, the symmetry between a rise or fall in the price of a stock in log terms becomes even more irrelevant since the value of the option does not move smoothly through all levels of the stock.

3. *The return we require.* Typically, the return we seek is related to our risk; if we take twice the risk, we want twice the return, and so forth. Since the average stock provides a total return of about 12% a year, for an option with a relative volatility of 800%, we'd want a return of 96% a year (800% × 12%). (Of course, for holding periods shorter than a year, we'd expect proportionally smaller returns.)

With these three pieces of information, we can easily calculate the price at which the option is likely to deliver the desired return.

PRICING THE OPTION FOR THE BUYER

Assume the expected value of a call at expiration is $3.00 and that a return of 20% is desired. Clearly, the call would have to be priced at $2.50 (before commissions) to provide that return, a simple calculation.

PRICING THE OPTION FOR THE SELLER

The buyer's investment is the price of the option. A seller's investment, in contrast, is the margin that must be posted. A seller, then, must calculate his return not against the price for which he sells the option but against the margin he must post. If margin amounts to $6 and the option was expected to be worth $3 at expiration, to earn 20%, the seller would have to sell the option for $4.20. (The seller must earn 20% on the $6 margin, or $1.20. Since he will have to buy back the option for $3, he must sell it for $1.20 more, or for $4.20.)

Note, however, that the seller's risk and the buyer's risk are not equal. The seller's loss is potentially unlimited whereas the buyer's loss is limited to the original cost of the option. It seems logical, then, to assume that the seller's risk is greater, but it's the other way around. Because the seller must put up a greater amount of capital than the buyer, the seller's leverage—or risk—is less. (A $1 price change in a $3 option represents a 33% price change for the buyer, but measured against $6 of margin it represents only a 16% change for the seller.) Thus, the return on investment targeted by the seller is almost always less than the return targeted by the buyer.

PRICING THE OPTION FOR THE COVERED WRITER

Risk. Whereas the risk in a naked option is always many times greater than the risk in the stock itself, a covered writing position, which includes both the stock and the call, usually has about half the risk of the stock. Consequently, the covered writer's fair rate of return will be substantially less than either the buyer or seller of the call. (The average call has a relative volatility of 1,000%, 10 times the average stock; the average covered call position has a relative volatility of 55%.)

Value at Expiration. The value at expiration of a covered writing position is not the value of the call, but the value of the entire position, which is equal to the value of the stock less the call, which must be bought back.

The Investment. The covered writer's investment is the cost basis of the position, equal to the cost of the stock reduced by the premium received from the sale of the call.

What Price the Call? If, for example, the expected value of a covered call position at expiration is $21 and the target return on investment for the period the option will be outstanding is 5%, we can calculate that our cost basis for the position must be $20. So if the price of the stock was $22, including commissions, the call must be sold for $2 net of commissions.

ITERATION

Sharp-eyed readers will have noted that a price for an option cannot be derived directly since the leverage, or risk, of an option changes with its price. An option worth $4 at expiration would have risen 100% if it originally cost $2 but only 33% if it originally cost $3. As the risk changes, the required return changes with it. So, we must find the price that provides a return indicated by the risk, which in turn depends on the original price. Thus we must test different prices until we find one that offers a return in line with the risk. As you will see from the examples and worksheets in this chapter, the process is not a difficult one.

CALLS VERSUS PUTS

Since stock prices tend to skew toward higher values, it is easy to understand that calls will have a greater value at expiration than puts.

SUMMARY

Risk and volatility are not one and the same. Risk, as the word implies, is a measure of the potential for unfavorable results. Volatility is a measure of both favorable and unfavorable results. The two are not always proportional; risk must be measured separately from volatility.

If an investor is to receive adequate compensation for risk, a naked buyer must buy an option for less than the option is likely to be worth at expiration, a naked seller must sell it for more than it is likely to be worth at expiration, and a covered writer can sell it for yet another price. Black-Scholes and similar models tend to set a value on the option at what it will be worth at expiration, a price at which neither the naked writer nor the naked seller can expect to earn a fair return. At that price, however, covered writers can typically earn a fabulous return.

PRICING OPTIONS BASED ON TRADITIONAL METHODS OF DETERMINING RISK VERSUS "NEGATIVE" RISK

The only difference between evaluating an option based on traditional methods of measuring risk and on "negative" risk is in the way risk is calculated. In traditional methods, the leverage of the option (i.e., the percent change in the price of the option compared to the percent change in the price of the stock) is tested at all stock prices and weighted by the probability of each price occurring. Thus, if the original price of the stock was $40 and the original price of a long call was $1, assuming that at expiration of the option the stock was likely to be at only two prices, $30 or $50, the call's leverage would be calculated as follows:

Price	Proba-bility	Percentage Change in Stock	Percentage Change in Option	Leverage	Weighted Leverage (Leverage × Probability)
$30	40%	−25%	−100%	4.0	1.6
$50	60%	+25%	+1,000%	40.0	24.0
				Total:	25.6

This call would then be considered to be 25.6 times as risky as the stock.

To calculate "negative" risk, we'd look only at prices at which there would be a loss. The leverage of the call would be calculated as follows:

	Stock Price	Probability	Potential Loss	Weighted Loss	Weighted Loss versus Original Investment
Stock:	$30	40%	$10	$4.00	10%
Call:	$30	40%	$ 1	$0.40	40%

As the risk of loss in this option is 40% in contrast to a 10% risk of loss in the stock, the option is four times as risky.

(*Note:* These illustrations are only to demonstrate the two methods of determining risk. Do not construe the differences in leverage indicated here as indicative of the differences typically determined by the two methods. A comparison of the risk and option values indicated by the two methods for a real life situation will be found in Exhibit 10.2 later in this chapter.)

As you review these figures, you will find that evaluating risk entirely with respect to the potential for loss rather than with respect to total volatility, which includes both the "risk" of profit as well as the risk of loss, not only is intuitively more logical, but it offers certain side benefits, as well.

In Exhibits 10.1a and 10.1b, you'll see how the origin of stock values, option values, and "negative" risk are easily illustrated by means of a simple, schematic diagram. In addition, and rather more important, the simplicity and speed of evaluating securities on the basis of "negative" risk becomes evident. (Indeed, at the end of this chapter, in Appendix 10-B, instead of five separate programs for evaluating options for call buying and writing, put buying and writing, and covered call writing, which are required in traditional methods, you'll find a single program based on "negative" risk, and this one program is but two-thirds the size of just one of the others.)

Exhibit 10.1a Valuing a Stock Based on "Negative" Risk

	A	B	C	D	E	F	G
			Price Change				
	Stock Price	Proba- bility	($)	Weighted (B × C)		Negative Risk	
	$25	0%	($5)	($0.00)	∧ E	∧ Long	
	$26	2%	($4)	($0.08)	x	| Position	
	$27	6%	($3)	($0.18)	p	|	
	$28	10%	($2)	($0.20)	'	|	
	$29	15%	($1)	($0.15)	d	∨	
Stock->	$30	25%	$0	$0.00			
	$31	16%	$1	$0.16	V	∧ Short	
	$32	12%	$2	$0.24	a	| Position	
	$33	8%	$3	$0.24	l	|	
	$34	5%	$4	$0.20	u	|	
	$35	1%	$5	$0.05	∨ e	∨	
					$.28	$.61	$.89

Column B: The probability of the stock being at the price shown in Column A at expiration of the option.

Column C: **Change in price of the stock.** (By working with the change in price rather than the price which appears in Column A, calculations are substantially simplified.)

Column D: The product of Columns B and C is equal to the weighted probable price change at each stock price.

Column E: **The expected price change in the stock.** The sum of Column D equals the probable change in the price of the stock at expiration of the option. Here, a rise of $0.28 is expected, so the expected value of the stock would be $30.28.

Column F: **The negative risk in a long position in the stock** . . . is the loss that would be suffered at lower prices multiplied by the probability of lower prices occurring. Here, for example, we simply take the sum of the weighted changes (Column D) for prices below $30. The negative risk here, then, can be expressed as $0.61, or 2.0% of the original price of the stock.

Exhibit 10.1a Continued

Column G: **The negative risk in a short position**. The risk in a short position is the loss that would be suffered at higher prices, here at prices above $30. In this stock, it is $0.89, or 3.0% of the original price of the stock.

If the common stock pays a dividend, the range over which negative risk occurs in a long position is reduced by the dividend (e.g., if the stock was $30 and paid a $1.50 dividend prior to expiration of the option under evaluation, the holder would be exposed to loss only if the stock dropped below $28.50.) Conversely, a short position would suffer a loss at prices above $28.50.

EVALUATING OPTIONS BASED ON "NEGATIVE" RISK

In Exhibit 10.1b we've added options to the evaluation. This schematic diagram shows clearly how the value of an option and its "negative" risk is derived.

Explanation of Exhibit 10.1b

Stock Price: $30   Strike Price: $32

Columns J & K: **Values of Options at Expiration**. An option's expected value is equal to the sum of the weighted tangible values of the option. For this call, that's $0.08 + $0.10 + $0.03, or $0.21. For the put, whose weighted tangible values are shown in brackets ( ), it's $1.93.

Columns L & O: **"Negative" risk in Long Options**. The "negative" risk in a long option occurs over the price range where its tangible value is zero (the price range where the loss is total) plus the price range where the tangible value is less than the cost of the option (the price range wherein a partial loss occurs).

Exhibit 10.1b Evaluating Options Based on "Negative" Risk

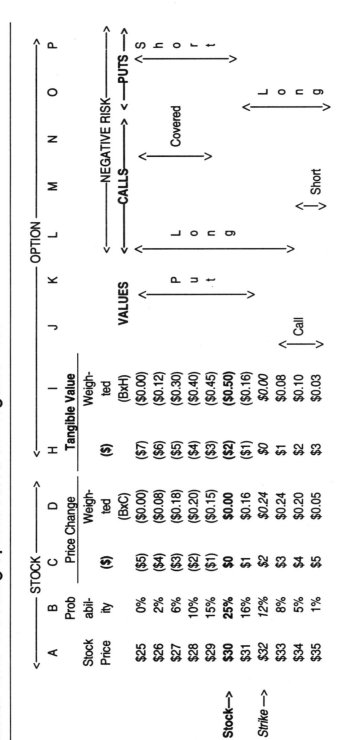

	A	B	C	D		H	I
		Prob-	Price Change	Weigh-		Tangible Value	Weigh-
	Stock	abil-		ted			ted
	Price	ity	($)	(BxC)		($)	(BxH)
	$25	0%	($5)	($0.00)		($7)	($0.00)
	$26	2%	($4)	($0.08)		($6)	($0.12)
	$27	6%	($3)	($0.18)		($5)	($0.30)
	$28	10%	($2)	($0.20)		($4)	($0.40)
	$29	15%	($1)	($0.15)		($3)	($0.45)
Stock—>	$30	25%	$0	$0.00		($2)	($0.50)
	$31	16%	$1	$0.16		($1)	($0.16)
Strike —>	$32	12%	$2	$0.24		$0	$0.00
	$33	8%	$3	$0.24		$1	$0.08
	$34	5%	$4	$0.20		$2	$0.10
	$35	1%	$5	$0.05		$3	$0.03

Columns J–P: OPTION VALUES — J (Call), K (Put), L (Long), M (Short), N (Covered), O (Long), P (Short); CALLS and PUTS grouped under NEGATIVE RISK.

Explanation of 10.1b Continued

Note: To calculate the "negative" risk in a long option position, it is not necessary to go through the long, step-by-step procedure shown in Exhibit 10.1b. All we have to do is multiply the the cost of the option by the probability of the stock being at any price at which either a total or partial loss occurs and subtract from that any values that would be recovered at those prices. For example, if we assume that this call cost $1.50, the buyer of this call would suffer a loss if the price of the stock, at expiration, was below the strike price plus the cost of the call, that is, below $33.50. The probability of the stock being below $33.50 in this diagram is 94%. Multiplying 94% x $1.50, the price of the call, give us $1.41, which is the potential loss the buyer faces over that price range. However, within this price range $0.08 would be recovered (if the stock were at $33), so the "negative" risk in this long call would be $1.33 ($1.41 - $0.08). Taken as a percentage of the original price, the risk amounts to 89% ($1.41/$1.50). Here are the calculations for these options:

	Long Call	Long Put
Price range over which option buyer will lose money (Strike: $32; Premium: $1.50):	Below $33.50	Above $30.50
Probability of the stock being within this range:	94%	42%
Potential loss (before recovery of tangible value) . . . Probability × $1.50 premium:	$1.41	$0.63
Tangible value that will be recovered within this price range:	.08	.16
"Negative" risk:	$1.33	$0.47
"Negative" risk as a percentage of the premium:	89%	31%

Columns M, N & P: **"Negative" risk in Short Options.** The "negative" risk for a seller of an option occurs over the price range at expiration where we expect the tangible value of the option to be greater than the option premium. Of course, that risk over this range is offset by the premium the seller received.

Explanation of 10.1b Continued

Here, too, we can shortcut the process. We take a sum of the weighted tangible values of the option over the price range that a loss would occur and subtract from that the portion of the option premium that would be earned in this price range, which we find, as above, by multiplying the total probability of the stock being at prices where the position would suffer a loss by the option premium. For example, a seller of this call who received $1.50 when the call was struck at $32 would suffer a loss if the stock ended above $33.50. The weighted tangible values of the call at prices above that adds to $0.13. The probability of the call being above $33.50 is 6%, so the weighted premium that would be earned above this price is $0.09 (6% x $1.50). The net "negative" risk for the seller of this call then is $0.04 ($0.13 - $0.09). To sell this call, the seller would have to post margin of $4. The "negative" risk in this call expressed as a percentage of the margin the seller must post is 1% ($0.04/$4.00). Here are the calculations for these short option positions:

	Naked Call	Covered Call	Naked Put
Price range over which seller will lose money (Stock: $30; Strike: $32; Premium: $1.50):	Above $33.50	Below $28.50	Below $30.50
Weighted value that will be lost within this price range:	.13	.46	1.77
Probability of the stock being within this range:	6%	18%	58%
Premium that would be recovered within this range . . . (Probability × $1.50 premium):	.09	.27	.87
"Negative" risk:	$0.04	$0.19	$0.90
Original investment:	(margin) $4.00	$28.50	(margin) $6.00
"Negative" risk as a percentage of original investment:	1%	.7%	15%

Explanation of Exhibit 10.1b Continued

Leverage. The volatility of an option position is equal to the volatility of the underlying stock multiplied by the option's leverage. Its leverage is measured by comparing its negative risk to the stock's negative risk. Bullish option positions (long calls, covered calls, short puts) are compared to the negative risk in a bullish position in the stock, bearish option positions (short calls, long puts) are compared to the negative risk in a bearish position in the stock. In the explanation of Exhibit 10.1a, we found the negative risk in a long stock position was 2% and it was 3% in a short stock position. The leverage of these option positions would be:

	"Negative" Risk in		
	Option	Stock	Leverage
Bullish Positions:			
Long Call:	89%	2%	44.50x
Covered Call:	.7%	2%	.35x
Short Put:	15%	2%	7.50x
Bearish Positions:			
Short Call:	1%	3%	.33x
Long Put:	33%	3%	11.00x

As you have seen in Exhibit 10.1b, long calls and puts, covered calls, and short calls and puts can all be evaluated in a single spread sheet. Cell formulas for constructing a Lotus spread sheet that will make these calculations will be found in Appendix 10.B. In contrast, five separate spread sheets are required—one each for long calls, long puts, covered calls, short calls and short puts—when we evaluate options by traditional methods. These are all described in Appendix 10.A.

How calls and puts are evaluated using traditional methods is illustrated in the Exhibits listed below. Call Buying was split into three separate Exhibits (10.3a, 10.3b and 10.3c) to make it possible to follow the derivation of the values step by step. Values for other positions using traditional methods are derived similarly but are combined into one Exhibit. You can replicate the values in these exhibits on your computer by constructing the Lotus spread sheets in Appendix 10.A.

	Exhibit
Call Buying:	
Expected value	10.3a
The Buyer's leverage (Risk)	10.3b
Appropriate Price for a Buyer	10.3c
Call Selling	10.4
Covered Writing	10.5
Put Buying	10.6
Put Selling	10.7

Exhibit 10.2 compares the option values we found when we evaluated the calls and puts described here by traditional methods (as we did in Exhibits 10.3–10.7) and based on "negative" risk.

Exhibit 10.2 Comparing Option Values: Traditional Methods versus "Negative" Risk

Stock Price: $30
Strike Price: $30
Relative Volatility of Stock: 100%

	Based on Traditional Methods		Based on Negative Risk	
	Price	Relative Volatility	Price	Relative Volatility
CALL				
Value at Expiration:	$2.96			
Appropriate Price for Buying:	$2.33	895%	$2.36	870%
Appropriate Price for Selling:	4.01	528%	3.53	250%
Black-Scholes Price:	*2.98*			
Appropriate Price for Covered Writing:	2.40	45%	2.47	55%
Value of Covered Position at Expiration:	$28.07			
PUT				
Value at Expiration:	$1.88			
Appropriate Price for Buying:	$1.45	1017%	$1.48	902%
Appropriate Price for Selling:	2.60	342%	2.26	169%
Black-Scholes Price:	*1.82*			

Here are the differences:

Strategy	Negative Risk versus Traditional Evaluation
Naked Option Buying	No real difference
Naked Option Selling	Lower risk—so lower prices
Covered Option Writing	Slightly higher risk—so slightly higher prices

1. Traditional methods of measuring risk overstate the risk of the seller. Since higher prices are demanded when risk is conceived to be higher, this may explain, in part, why option writers typically make out better than buyers.

2. Note how attractive covered writing is relative to other option strategies. If a covered writer can earn a fair return selling this call for **$2.47**, he can obviously earn a superior return selling it for **$2.98**, the price indicated by the Black-Scholes model, a price many option traders are guided by. Were he to sell this call for **$3.53**, the price appropriate for a naked writer, his risk would become lower still while he looked forward to earning an indicated annual return of 22%. In practice, such returns appear to be realizable on a consistent basis.

3. Put values for comparable options are always lower than call values. This is because the probability of higher stock prices is greater than the probability of lower stock prices.

4. Returns on investment for selling naked options are based on initial out-of-pocket margin requirements before commissions. An average of the initial margin and final margin may be used in its place. Were

average margin used, indicated prices for calls would be slightly higher and indicated prices for puts would be slightly lower.

Exhibit 10.3a Valuing Calls Based on Traditional Methods

Days to Expiration:	120
Strike Price:	$30
Initial Price of Stock:	$30
Relative Volatility of Stock:	100%

(Before Commissions)

A	B	C	D
			Weighted Value
Stock ($)	Probability	Position's Value	B × C
$18	0.5%	$0.00	0.00
$19	0.6%	$0.00	0.00
$20	1.0%	$0.00	0.00
. . .	. . .	. . .	. . .
$27	6.2%	$0.00	0.00
$28	6.6%	$0.00	0.00
$29	6.7%	$0.00	0.00
$30	6.7%	$0.00	0.00
$31	6.5%	$1.00	0.06
$32	6.1%	$2.00	0.12
$33	5.6%	$3.00	0.17
. . .	. . .	. . .	. . .
$53	0.1%	$23.00	0.02
$54	0.1%	$24.00	0.01
$55	0.0%	$25.00	0.01
TOTALS	1.00		$2.96

Exhibit 10.3b Determining a Call Buyer's Leverage by Traditional Methods

A	B	C	D	E	F	G	H
		Posi-	Weighted	Percentage			Weighted
Stock	Proba-	tion's	Value	Change in Value of		Leverage	Leverage
($)	bility	Value	B × C	Stock	Psn.	F/E	B × G
$18	0.5%	$0.00	0.00	−40%	−100%	2.5	0.01
$19	0.6%	$0.00	0.00	−37%	−100%	2.7	0.02
$20	1.0%	$0.00	0.00	−33%	−100%	3.0	0.03
. . .	. . .	. . .	. . .	. . .	. . .	. . .	. . .
$27	6.2%	$0.00	0.00	−10%	−100%	10.0	0.62
$28	6.6%	$0.00	0.00	−7%	−100%	15.0	0.99
$29	6.7%	$0.00	0.00	−3%	−100%	30.0	2.02
$30	6.7%	$0.00	0.00	0%	−100%		
$31	6.5%	$1.00	0.06	3%	−60%	17.9	1.16
$32	6.1%	$2.00	0.12	7%	−19%	2.9	0.17
. . .	. . .	. . .	. . .	. . .	. . .	. . .	. . .
$53	0.1%	$23.00	0.02	77%	831%	10.8	0.01
$54	0.1%	$24.00	0.01	80%	872%	10.9	0.01
$55	0.0%	$25.00	0.01	83%	912%	10.9	0.00
TOTALS	1.00		$2.96				8.95

Note: Cell formulas for a Lotus spreadsheet will be found in Appendix 10.A.

CHAPTER 10

Exhibit 10.3c Pricing a Call for a Buyer by Traditional Methods

		(calculations)	
a.	Relative Volatility of Stock:	100%	
b.	Option's Leverage:	8.95	
c.	Relative Volatility of Option:	895%	a × b
d.	Risk-Free Rate or Desired Return	12%	
e.	Desired Annualized Return*:	107%	c × d
f.	Desired Return for Period*:	27%	$(e+1)^{(120/365)}-1$
f.	Probable Value of Option at Expiration:	$2.96	
h.	Suggested Price:	$2.33	g/(1+f)
i.	PRICE DETERMINED BY ITERATION	$2.33	

* See explanation below:

d. Based on a 12% annualized return for a stock with a relative volatility of 100%. (See Chapter 7.) As the risk here is 8.95 times greater, the annualized return required is 8.95 times greater, or 107%.

e. The 120-day return, which compounds to 107% in 12 months (one year).

h. This is the suggested price ($2.33) the buyer should pay (ignoring commissions) if the $2.96 he expects the call to be worth when it expires is to provide the desired 20% return on investment.

i. The process for finding the price of the option that will deliver the desired return is "iterative." We must test different prices until we find one that provides a return appropriate to the risk. That's because the leverage, or risk, of the option changes as its price changes (i.e., a $1 change in price of an option that cost $2 is equivalent to a 50% change; if the option had cost $3, it would represent a 33% change) . . . so a change in price changes the risk, and that in turn changes the return we must earn to compensate for that altered level of risk. In this example, we went through this iterative process to arrive at the price of $2.33 for the call, and in doing so learned what its leverage was at that price.

The process is not as exhausting as this sounds, however. In the Lotus spreadsheet, the "Suggested Price" acts a guide toward reaching the right price for the option. The appropriate price for the option is found when the price that is entered on Line 72 (see Appendix 10.A) corresponds to the "Suggested Price," which appears on Line 71.

Since the leverage of the option changes with its cost, values that are input for the option at expiration and the price of the stock should be after commissions.

154

Exhibit 10.4   Valuing a Call Seller's Position by Traditional Methods

A	B	C	D	E	F	G	H
			Weighted	Percentage change in Value of		Lever-	Weighted
Stock	Proba-	Position's	Value			age	Leverage
($)	bility	Value	B × C	Stock	Psn.	F/E	B × G
$18	0.5%	$0.00	0.00	–40%	62%	1.5	0.01
$19	0.6%	$0.00	0.00	–37%	62%	1.7	0.01
$20	1.0%	$0.00	0.00	–33%	62%	1.9	0.02
. . .	. . .	. . .	. . .	. . .	. . .	. . .	. . .
$53	0.1%	$23.00	0.02	77%	–322%	4.2	0.00
$54	0.1%	$24.00	0.01	80%	–338%	4.2	0.00
$55	0.0%	$25.00	0.01	83%	–355%	4.3	0.00
TOTALS	1.00		$2.96				5.28

VALUE OF CALL FROM SELLER'S PERSPECTIVE

		(calculations)
a.	Relative Volatility of Stock:	100%
b.	Option's Leverage:	5.28
c.	Relative Volatility of Option:	528% a × Bb
d.	Risk-Free Rate or Desired Return:	12%
e.	Desired Annualized Return:	63% c × Dd
f.	Desired Return for Period:	18% $(e+1)\wedge(120/365)-1$
g.	Probable Value of Option at Expiration:	$2.96
h.	Suggested Price:	$4.04 f × $6.00* + G
i.	PRICE DETERMINED BY ITERATION	$4.01

* Initial outlay for margin.

Exhibit 10.5 Valuing a Covered Writing Position by Traditional Methods

A	B	C	D	E	F	G	H
		Posi-	Weighted	Percentage		Lever-	Weighted
Stock	Proba-	tion's	Value	Change in Value of		age	Leverage
($)	bility	Value	B × C	Stock	Psn.	F/E	B × G
$18	0.5%	18	0.09	–40%	–34%	0.8	0.00
$19	0.6%	19	0.11	–37%	–30%	0.8	0.00
$20	1.0%	20	0.21	–33%	–26%	0.8	0.01
. . .	. . .	. . .	. . .	. . .	. . .	. . .	. . .
$53	0.1%	30	0.02	77%	10%	0.1	0.00
$54	0.1%	30	0.02	80%	10%	0.1	0.00
$55	0.0%	30	0.01	83%	10%	0.1	0.00
TOTALS	1.00		$28.07				0.45

VALUE OF CALL FROM A COVERED WRITER'S PERSPECTIVE

			(calculations)
a.	Relative Volatility of Stock:	100%	
b.	Call's Leverage:	0.45	
c.	Relative Volatility of Call:	45%	a × b
d.	Risk-Free Interest Rate or Desired Return:	12%	
e.	Desired Annualized Return:	54%	c × Dd
f.	Desired Return for Three Months:	2%	$(e+1)^{\wedge}(120/365)-1$
g.	Price of Stock:	$30.00	
h.	Net Cost of Position:	$27.60	g – m
i.	Probable Value of Position at Expiration:	$28.35	
j.	Plus Dividends:	0.00	
k.	Total:	$28.35	i + j
l.	Suggested Price of Call:	$2.21	g – k/(1 + f)
m.	PRICE DETERMINED BY ITERATION	$2.40	

Exhibit 10.6 Valuing a Put Buyer's Position by Traditional Methods

A Stock ($)	B Proba- bility	C Posi- tion's Value	D Weighted Value B × C	E Percentage Change in Value of Stock	F Psn.	G Lever- age F/E	H Weighted Leverage B × G
$18	0.5%	$12.00	0.07	−40%	674%	16.9	0.09
$19	0.6%	$11.00	0.07	−37%	610%	16.6	0.10
$20	1.0%	$10.00	0.10	−33%	545%	16.4	0.17
. . .	. . .	. . .	. . .	. . .	. . .	. . .	. . .
$53	0.1%	$0.00	0.00	77%	−100%	1.3	0.00
$54	0.1%	$0.00	0.00	80%	−100%	1.3	0.00
$55	0.0%	$0.00	0.00	83%	−100%	1.2	0.00
TOTALS	1.00		$1.88				10.17

VALUE OF PUT FROM BUYER'S PERSPECTIVE

			(calculations)
a.	Relative Volatility of Stock:	100%	
b.	Option's Leverage:	10.17	
c.	Relative Volatility of Option:	1017%	a × b
d.	Risk-Free Rate or Desired Return:	12%	
e.	Desired Annualized Return:	122%	c × d
f.	Desired Return for Three Months:	30%	(e+1)^(120/365)−1
g.	Probable Value of Option at Expiration:	$1.88	
h.	Price That Will Provide Desired Return:	$1.45	g/(1 + f)
i.	PRICE DETERMINED BY ITERATION	$1.45	

Exhibit 10.7   Valuing a Put Seller's Position by Traditional Methods

A	B	C	D	E	F	G	H
		Posi-	Weighted	Percentage		Lever-	Weighted
Stock	Proba-	tion's	Value	Change in Value of		age	Leverage
($)	bility	Value	B × C	Stock	Psn.	F/E	B × G
$18	0.5%	$12.00	0.07	−40%	−160%	4.0	0.02
$19	0.6%	$11.00	0.07	−37%	−144%	3.9	0.02
$20	1.0%	$10.00	0.10	−33%	−127%	3.8	0.04
. . .	. . .	. . .	. . .	. . .	. . .	. . .	. . .
$53	0.1%	$0.00	0.00	77%	40%	0.5	0.00
$54	0.1%	$0.00	0.00	80%	40%	0.5	0.00
$55	0.0%	$0.00	0.00	83%	40%	0.5	0.00
TOTALS	1.00		$1.88				3.42

VALUE OF PUT FROM SELLER'S PERSPECTIVE

		(calculations)
a.	Relative Volatility of Stock:	100%
b.	Option's Leverage:	3.42
c.	Relative Volatility of Option:	342% a × b
d.	Risk-Free Rate or Desired Return:	12%
e.	Desired Annualized Return:	41% c × d
f.	Desired Return for Three Months:	12% (e+1)^(120/365) −1
g.	Probable Value of Option at Expiration:	$1.88
h.	Price That Will Provide Desired Return:	$2.60 f × $6.00* + g
i.	PRICE DETERMINED BY ITERATION	$2.60

* Margin

APPENDIX 10.A
Lotus Worksheet for Valuing Options**
Based on Traditional Methods for Evaluating Risk

**Note*: This spreadsheet below may be set up to value calls, puts, or covered call positions for buyers or sellers using the cell formulas that appear at the bottom of this appendix.

—————————————Spreadsheet as it appears in Lotus—————————————

Line #	Stock	Price:	$32.00	OPTION VALUATION		Strike:	Margin: $6.40 $30.00		
3	A	B	C	D	E	F	G	H
4				Weighted			Lever	Weighted
5				Value			age	Leverage
6		Prob-	Posi-	B	% Change in		F	B
7	Stk	abil-	tion's	x	Value of		/	x
8	($)	ity	Value	C	Stock	Psn	E	G
9								
10	$18	0.0%	$18.00	0.01	–44%	–36%	0.8	0.00
11	$19	0.1%	$19.00	0.02	–41%	–33%	0.8	0.00
. . .	. . .	. . .	. . .	. . .	. . .	. . .	. . .	. . .
23	$31	7.2%	$30.00	2.17	–3%	7%	2.1	0.15
24	$32	7.2%	$30.00	2.17	0%	7%		
25	$33	7.0%	$30.00	2.11	3%	7%	2.1	0.15
. . .	. . .	. . .	. . .	. . .	. . .	. . .	. . .	. . .
46	$54	0.1%	$30.00	0.02	69%	7%	0.1	0.00
47	$55	0.0%	$30.00	0.01	72%	7%	0.1	0.00
48								
50	TOTALS	1.00		$29.00			0.68	

51								
52			VALUE OF CALL FROM COVERED WRITER'S PERSPECTIVE					
53								
54	A	B	C	D	E	F	G	H
56	Relative Volatility of Stock:					100%		

57	Position's Leverage:		0.68
58	Relative Volatility of Position:		68%
59			
60	Risk-Free Interest Rate:		12%
61	Desired Annualized Return:		8%
62	Desired Return for Three Months:		2%
63			
64	Price of Stock:		$32.00
65	Net Cost of Position:		$32.00
66			
67	Probable Value of Psn at Exp.:		$29.00
68	Plus Dividends:		0.00
69		Total:	$29.00
70			
71	Suggested Option Price:		$3.56
72	INPUT PRICE OF OPTION HERE——>		$3.47

————————————End of spreadsheet————————————

CELL FORMULAS
For Covered Writing

A10: See Appendix 10.A
B10: See Appendix 10.A
C10: @if(A10$G$2,$G$2,A10)
D10: +B10*C10
E10: +$A10/$C$2-1
F10: +C10/($C$2-$E$72)-1
G10: @IF(E100,@ABS(F10)/@ABS(E10)," ")
H10: +G10*B10

Copy above cell formulas down to Line 47, or lower if Columns A through H go lower.

B50: @SUM(B10..B47)
D50: @SUM(D10..D47)

H50:	@SUM(H10..H47)
E56:	Stock's relative volatility
E57:	+H50
E58:	+E56*E57
E60:	Interest rate or desired annual return
E61:	+E58*E60
E62:	(1+E61)^(# days to exp./365)-1
E64:	+C2
E65:	+E64-E72
E67:	+D50
E68:	Div'ds to be rec'd before expiration
E69:	+E67+E68
E71:	+E64-E69/(1+E62)
E72:	Enter option price here until it equals E71

For Call Buying, change these cells:

C10:	@IF(A10G$2,0,A10-$G$2)
F10:	+C10/$E$65-1
F64:	OMIT
F65:	OMIT
F68:	OMIT
F69:	OMIT
E71:	+D50/(1+E62)
E72:	Enter price here until it equals E71
	End of worksheet. Omit cells below.

For Call Selling, change these cells:

C10:	@IF(A10G$2,0,A10-$G$2)
F10:	($E$65-C10)/$G$1
F64:	OMIT
F65:	OMIT
F68:	OMIT

F69:	OMIT
E71:	+D50+(E62+G1)
E72:	Enter price here until it equals E71
	End of worksheet. Omit cells below.

For Put Buying, change these cells:

C10:	@IF(A10$G$2,0,$G$2–A10)
F10:	+C10/$E$65–1
F64:	OMIT
F65:	OMIT
F68:	OMIT
F69:	OMIT
E71:	+D50/(1+E62)
E72:	Enter price here until it equals E71
	End of worksheet. Omit cells below.

For Put Selling, change these cells:

C10:	@IF(A10$G$2,0,$G$2-A10)
F10:	($E$65-C10)/$G$1
F64:	OMIT
F65:	OMIT
F68:	OMIT
F69:	OMIT
E71:	+D50+(E62∗G1)
E72:	Enter price here until it equals E71
	End of worksheet. Omit cells below.

When using this spreadsheet, remember that the relative volatility of the stock is the estimated future volatility. In addition, the price of the stock may be skewed, if desired, to reflect your forecast for the future absolute or relative price movement.

APPENDIX 10.B
Lotus Worksheet for Valuing Options**
Based on "Negative" Risk

(Values to be input are shown in **bold**)

	A	B	C	D	E	F	G	H	I	J	K
	Stock	**$36.00**	Div'd	**$3.00** Rel Vol		**100%** Rqd Return		**12.0%**		
3			#Days	**120** Strike:		**$30.00** Margin		**$7.20**		
4	Option test price:			**$8.60**						

Note: "Est'd Value" (below) is the estimated value of the stock or option at expiration. The appropriate price at which to buy or sell an option for a particular strategy is indicated when the "Option test price" on line 4 equals the "Suggest(ed) Price" for that strategy on lines 7–11 in column E.

	A	B	C	D	E	F	G	H	I	J	K
						Relative					Return
5				Est'd	Suggest	Volatility		Negative Risk		Desired	for
6				Value	Price	Psn	Opt	($s	(%)	Lvg	Period
7	Call (Long)			$7.77	$6.50	597%		$3.23	37.5%	5.97	19.4%
8	Call (Short)				$8.59	325%	272%	$2.34	27.2%	2.72	11.4%
9	Put (Long)			$0.44	$0.31	1510%		$8.16	94.9%	15.10	40.5%
10	Put (Short)				$0.44	1%	0%	$0.00	0.0%	0.00	0.0%
11	Cov Call Psn			$29.56	$6.55	9%		$0.16	0.6%	0.09	0.4%
12	Stock (Long)			$37.33				$2.26	6.3%		
13	Stock (Short)							$3.59	10.0%		

	A	B	C	D	E	F	G
15	Stock	Prob-		Stock	Option		Option
16	Incre-	abil-	Wt'd	Cum'l	Incre-	Wt'd	Cum'l
17	ment	ity	Value	Value	ment	Value	Value
18	-34.90	0.0%	0.00	0.00	-28.90	0.00	0.00
19	-33.80	0.0%	0.00	0.00	-27.80	0.00	0.00
20	-32.70	0.0%	0.00	0.00	-26.70	0.00	0.00
...	...	...	...	...	...	...	...
40	-8.50	2.9%	-0.24	-0.93	-2.50	-0.07	-0.39
41	-7.40	3.6%	-0.27	-1.20	-1.40	-0.05	-0.44
42	-6.30	4.3%	-0.27	-1.47	-0.30	-0.01	-0.45
43	-5.20	5.0%	-0.26	-1.72	0.80	0.04	-0.41
44	-4.10	5.5%	-0.23	-1.95	1.90	0.10	-0.31
45	-3.00	5.9%		-1.95	3.00	0.18	-0.13

46	−1.90	6.1%	−0.12	−2.07	4.10	0.25	0.12
47	−0.80	6.2%	−0.05	−2.12	5.20	0.32	0.44
48	0.30	6.1%	0.02	−2.10	6.30	0.38	0.82
49	1.40	5.9%	0.08	−2.02	7.40	0.44	1.26
. . .	. . .	. . .	. . .	. . .	. . .	. . .	. . .
77	30.00	0.0%	0.01	1.42	36.00	0.01	7.23
78	31.10	0.0%	0.01	1.42	37.10	0.01	7.24
79	32.20	0.0%	0.01	1.43	38.20	0.01	7.25
Etc.							

CELL FORMULAS

D7: +G79−@MIN(G18..G79)

E7: +D7/(1+K7)

F7: +$F$2*J7

H7: @VLOOKUP($E$4,$E$18..$R$79,13)*$E$4+@VLOOKUP(0,$E$18..$G$79

I7: +H7/$E$4

J7: +I7/$I$12

K7: ($I$2*F7+1)^($D$3/365)−1

E8: +D7+(K8*$I$3)

F8: +G8*$E$4/$I$3

G8: +$F$2*J8

H8: +G79−@VLOOKUP(E4+M18,E18..G79,2)−(1−@VLOOKUP(E4+M18, E18..R79 ,13))*E4

I8: +H8/$E$4

J8: +I8/$I$13

K8: ($I$2*F8+1)^($D$3/365)−1

D9: −@MIN(G18..G79)

E9: +D9/(1+K9)

F9: +$F$2*J9

H9: (1−@VLOOKUP(−$E$4+$M$18,$E$18..$R$79,13))*$E$4+(@MIN ($G$18.. $G$79)−@VLOOKUP(−$E$4+M18,$E$18..$G$79,2))

I9: H9/$E$4

J9: +I9/$I$12

K9: ($I$2*F9+1)^($D$3/365)−1

E10: +D9+(K10*$I$3)

F10: +G10*$E$4/$I$3

G10: +$F$2*J10

H10: -@VLOOKUP(-$E$4,$E$18..$R$79,13)*$E$4-@VLOOKUP(-$E$4, $E$18.. $G$79,2)

I10: +H10/$E$4

J10: +I10/$I$13

K10: ($I$2*F10+1)^($D$3/365)-1

D11: +D12-D7+D2

E11: +B2-D11/(1+K11)

F11: +$F$2*J11

H11: -@VLOOKUP(-E4,A18..D79,3)-@VLOOKUP(-E4,A18..R79,17)*E4

I11: +H11/(B2-E4)

J11: +I11/I12

K11: ($I$2*F11+1)^($D$3/365)-1

D12: @SUM(C18..C79)+B2

H12: -D47-R47*D2

I12: +H12/$B$2

H13: +D79-D47+(1-R47)*D2

I13: +H13/$B$2

A18: Price Increments   use as small an increment as desired

B18: From log-normal table   copy down

C18: +A18*B18   copy down

D18: +C18

E18: +M18-$F$3

D19: +D18+C19   copy down

E18: +A18+$D$2-$F$3   copy down

F18: +E18*B18   copy down

G18: +F18

G19: +G18+F19   copy down

EFFECTIVE INVESTMENT STRATEGIES

Covered Call Writing: Protecting Your Stocks and Boosting Your Income Too

At last we turn to the fine points of covered call writing, one of two option strategies likely to pay off consistently. This strategy not only cuts the risk of holding common stocks by about half, but typically enhances investment returns as well.

EXCITEMENT

What generates excitement in the stock market is sharply rising earnings, and many companies go to unusual lengths to provide investors with just that, or when not otherwise possible, at least the illusion of it. Early in my career as a securities analyst, soon after being assigned to follow the giant conglomerate ITT, Bob Savage, then head of that company's investor relations department, phoned to introduce himself: "Hi," he boomed, "I'm Vice President in charge of the Price Of The Stock."

As I soon discovered, Bob wasn't joking. In his view, the price of the stock was his responsibility, which meant feeding investors news that would keep them excited and the stock hopping, no easy task since the company wasn't cooperating. Profits were in a prolonged slide. But Bob was creative. Each quarter, at a special analysts' meeting at which the period's earnings were announced, he explained why, if not for ridiculously inflexible SEC accounting rules, instead of falling profits, ITT would have reported the higher earnings it really achieved.

The buzzwords companies adopt to persuade investors that they're "with it" are just as funny. In the early 1980s, neither ITT nor any respectable company would consider making a presentation to the financial community without mentioning "synergism" at least once. (I counted the word 117 times that year, but I missed a lot of meetings.) A year later, synergism was out and "systems" was in. Nuts and bolts vendors, that year, became manufacturers of fastening "systems."

Perhaps the most inventive use of that particular buzzword goes to Standex, a New Hampshire-based conglomerate, which managed to yoke that buzzword to the nation's then emerging concern about the environment. Its annual report that year outlined, with not quite modest adjectives, the progress of its "Environmental Systems" Group. Fearing I had missed an acquisition, or had lost touch with a portion of that company that had never before been conspicuously mentioned, I phoned Standex's director of investor relations, a short, jolly fellow with a well-honed sense of humor. "Sol," I asked, after a brief chit chat, "did you make an acquisition you didn't tell me about?"

"An acquisition?" he repeated, clearly a bit confused. "Oh," he chuckled, when directed to the paragraph in question, "we bought that company years ago . . . it's the sheet metal firm that makes ducts for air conditioning systems."

But any award for this sort of verbal legerdemain should probably go to John Ong, head of Goodrich. For over a half dozen years, it was John's distasteful task to report not a series of earnings declines, but a series of major corporate blunders, one more disastrous than another. Yet, the way he orchestrated the disclosures, they sounded as if the disasters were part of Goodrich's long-term strategic plan.

WHAT IS COVERED CALL WRITING?

Clearly, if it's excitement you crave, there are enough of these spellbinders around to satisfy everyone's taste. But covered call writing is not exciting . . . unless you consider a strategy that's low in risk and throws off excellent and consistent returns exciting. If that's the kind of excitement you crave, then covered call writing is for you.

Covered call writing, also called buy/writes, combines the purchase of common stock and the sale of one call against each 100 shares. The position is "covered" because if the call is exercised, you may simply deliver your stock to fulfill your obligation. (*Note:* Although you have the obligation to deliver stock if the call is exercised, if you wish to keep your stock, you can usually buy back the call just before it expires or, as an alternate, buy additional shares and deliver those in its place. Either way, you make the same profit.)

Covered call writing is a bullish strategy because it does best if the stock is at or above the exercise price when the call expires. The call premium that the writer receives reduces the cost basis of the stock, so the position produces a profit even if the price of the stock remains flat, but even if it drops, there may be no loss at all, or at worst, a smaller loss than would be suffered if the call hadn't been written.

Assume, for example, that you bought a stock at $20 and sold a six-month call against it struck at the market (at $20) for $2 a share. Exhibit 11.1 shows a comparison of the profit or loss of the covered call position to your results if you had held the stock but hadn't written a call against it.

Exhibit 11.1 Covered Writing versus Holding Stock Uncovered

STOCK AT EXPIRATION:	$14	$16	$18	**$20**	$22	$24	$26
Percentage Gain/Loss:	–30%	–20%	–10%	0%	+10%	+20%	+30%

COVERED CALL POSITION (cost basis: $18):

	$14	$16	$18	**$20**	$22	$24	$26
Stock:	–$6	–$4	–$2	**$ 0**	+$2	+$4	+$6
Value of Call:	–	–	–	–	–$2	–$4	–$6
Call Premium:	+$2	+$2	+$2	+$2	+$2	+$2	+$2
Covered Call Position:	–$4	–$2	–$0	+$2	+$2	+$2	+$2
Percentage Gain/Loss:	–22%	–11%	0%	+11%	+11%	+11%	+11%

Notice that the covered writer does better if the stock rises by as much as 10%—or if it rises less, or falls. But if the stock were to rise more than 10% during the six-month period, the investor would do better holding the stock and not writing a call against it. The conclusion: if you can consistently pick stocks that rise sharply, don't write covered calls against them. Note, however, that by writing the call, you earn an 11% profit over the six-month period even if the stock doesn't rise—at sharply reduced risk (a covered writer's risk is only about half of an uncovered stockholder's). Moreover, at the end of the six months, you can write a second call and so earn over 22% a year on a stock that doesn't rise at all . . . plus dividends. The average stock, in contrast, earns only 10% to 12% a year, including dividends.

THE REWARD/RISK RATIO

Notice how covered call writing shifts the reward/risk ratio solidly in your favor. In theory, investments are supposed to provide returns in proportion to their risk, the greater the risk the greater the return for taking that risk. What makes an investment attractive, then, is if it offers a greater return than would be expected for a given level of risk—or an equal return at less risk. Thus, if the average stock returns 12% a year, you'd expect covered writing, which has about half the risk, to return about 6%. In fact, covered writing generates as much as 18%, with not much more than half the risk.

> The average stock provides a return of 12% a year. As its relative volatility is 100%, its reward/risk ratio is 0.12 (12%/100%). Covered writing provides a return averaging 18% a year (or more). It has a relative volatility of 55%. Its reward/risk ratio is 0.33 (18%/55%), almost three times as great.

Let's look at actual prices and see why covered writing is so much more attractive. In Chapter 10, you will recall, we found that we could sell a call for far less than the "fair" price indicated by Black-Scholes and still establish a covered call position with a reward/risk ratio of 0.12. In Exhibit 11.2, we find that at the Black-Scholes' price, the covered call's reward/risk ratio is 0.26 . . . and at the price at which a "naked" seller must sell a call to earn a profit, the ratio soars to 0.60, five times better than an uncovered stock offers. Notice, too, that at the price Black-Scholes designates as "fair," the covered writer not only has less than half the risk of the uncovered stock owner, but also can expect to earn a return that is slightly better. By selling the call at the price a naked call writer would demand, his risk is even less while the expected return is almost double.

All of this helps explain why, as mentioned in Chapter 10, returns for covered call writing in excess of 20% are achievable. While *Value Line Options* does not evaluate covered call positions entirely in line with the techniques recommended in this book, its recommendations have achieved an average return in excess of 20% a year over more than 15 years. Because option prices move quickly, investors who follow these recommendations will not realize returns as high, but my personal experience has indicated that returns of 15% to 20% are achievable. The evaluation methods recommended in this book will help you identify the most attractive positions available in the market—or the best of the recommendations in Value Line.

Covered Call Writing

Exhibit 11.2 Evaluating Covered Call Writing Positions

STOCK Price: $30.00 Relative Volatility: 100%
CALL Strike: $30.00 Days to Expiration: 120

Expected Values at Expiration:
Covered Call Position: $28.07*
Stock, Alone: $31.11*

COVERED CALL POSITIONS Call price suggested by our model for ...	Call Price	Cost Basis of Covered Call Position	Return Expected Period	Annualized	Relative Volatility	Reward/ Risk Ratio
Covered Call Writing	$2.50	$27.50	2.1%	6.3%	54%	0.12
Naked Call Buying	$2.34	$27.66	1.5%	4.5%	56%	0.08
Naked Call Writing	$3.75	$26.25	6.9%	22.3%	37%	0.60
Black-Scholes Model	$2.98	$27.02	3.9%	12.1%	46%	0.26
STOCK ALONE			3.7%	11.7%	100%	0.12

Notes:

1. The expected value of the stock after 120 days is $31.11. At that price, the holder of the stock would earn 3.7% for the period or 12% annually—an indicated reward/risk ratio of 0.12.

2. The expected value of a covered call position at expiration can never be as great as the strike price of the call. At all higher stock prices, the covered writer receives only the strike price (here, $30); at lower prices, the position is worth less. The weighted average expected value of this covered writing position at expiration is $28.07.

* Plus dividends, if any.

THE THREE DEGREES OF BULLISHNESS

Although essentially a bullish strategy, covered writing can be tailored to provide different degrees of downside protection and allow different degrees of bullishness. With stock at $30, for example, a covered writer might choose from the calls shown in Exhibit 11.3.

Exhibit 11.3   Deciding on the Amount of Downside Protection

Strike	Premium	Cost Basis	Profit to Expect if Stock Is Unchanged	Profit if Stock Goes to Strike	Downside Protection
$35	$1.00	$29.00	3%	21%	3%
$30	3.00	27.00	11%	11%	10%
$25	5.50	24.50	2%	2%	18%

An aggressive covered writer would sell calls with strikes far above the price of the stock. These offer the maximum profit potential but have the least downside protection. Covered writers willing to take less risk will sell at-the-money calls. These are typically the most attractive: they provide an attractive combination of moderate appreciation potential and moderate downside protection. Covered writers wishing to minimize risk would write deep-in-the-money calls, which, though they provide substantial downside protection, allow minimal profit potential.

While writing far out-of-the-money and deep-in-the-money calls both have their place, these covered call positions suggest an ability on the part of the investor to call the market's direction. But neither takes full advantage of the hedge a covered call position offers nor does either cater to the fact that the single most likely price of a stock in the future is its price today. For the investor who isn't able to call the market successfully but wishes to maximize his returns over the long run without giving up reasonable downside protection, at-the-money or slightly in-the-money calls are the ones to write.

CHOOSING BETWEEN ALTERNATE POSITIONS

While we look for investment positions with superior reward/risk ratios, a superior reward/risk ratio alone won't satisfy every investment objective. Interest-bearing bank accounts, for example, have very high reward/risk ratios largely because their risk is so low. But the returns they offer are extremely modest. In addition to the reward/risk ratio, there are three other things to know about a covered call position we are considering:

1. Is the expected return within a range that is satisfactory?

2. How large a drop in the stock, percentage-wise, can be sustained before a loss results? (A loss results only if the stock drops by more than the call premium.)

3. How large a drop in the stock, percentage-wise, can be sustained yet still earn the full expected return? (The full return is earned if the stock, at expiration, is no lower than the strike; thus, if the stock is above the strike when the call is written, it has room to drop before the expected profit is reduced).

To make these calculations, plug in the price of the stock, dividends due to expiration, and the price, strike price, and month of expiration of the call as shown in Exhibit 11.4.

Cast your eye down Columns H, I, and J in Exhibit 11.4. The issues there appeared in a further screen of covered call candidates that had attractive reward/risk ratios on February 5, 1993. Notice that the first covered call position, combining the May 17 1/2 CMZ call, was quite attractive. With the stock $19.63, it offered an annualized return greater than 34%, more than 17% of loss protection, and the 34% return was safe even if the stock fell 11%. Not so attractive was the second position; although it offered wide loss and profit protection, the annualized profit potential (8%) didn't fit our requirements. On the other hand, the WWY March 30 call position offered a whopping 62% annualized return, but the absence of profit protection and the 5.4% downside protection weren't all we wished for even though the position had only a little more than a month to expiration. With the figures before you, it's easy to weed out positions that don't meet your requirements and select the best of those that do.

Exhibit 11.4 Covered Option Evaluation (Assuming Stock Price Is Unchanged at Expiration) 05-Feb-93

A	B	C	D*	E*	F	G	H	I	J
			Price		Dividend to	Profit to	Profit	Loss	Profit
Issue	M/E	Strike	Option	Stock	Expiration	Expiration	Annual	PROTECTION	
cmz	5	17.50	3.875	19.630	.18	8.8%	34.1%	17.2%	11%
mxs	7	7.50	2.625	9.875		3.4%	8.0%	26.6%	24%
pgr	5	35.00	1.625	35.125	.05	4.6%	17.0%	4.6%	0%
	5	35.00	3.250	35.125	.10	10.1%	39.8%	9.3%	0%
ujb	6	20.00	4.625	23.500		6.0%	17.2%	19.7%	15%
	7	20.00	5.375	23.500		10.3%	25.0%	22.9%	15%
wwy	5	30.00	1.250	30.000		4.3%	15.9%	4.2%	0%
	3	30.00	1.625	30.000		5.7%	62.2%	5.4%	0%
	6	30.00	2.625	30.000	.10	10.0%	29.7%	8.8%	0%
cu	5	30.00	2.250	27.500		8.9%	34.5%	8.2%	-9%
ca	6	30.00	0.875	26.625		3.4%	9.6%	3.3%	-13%
cns	5	15.00	2.875	17.375		3.4%	12.5%	16.5%	14%
	7	15.00	3.500	17.375		8.1%	19.3%	20.1%	14%
sgq	4	22.50	0.500	18.625		2.8%	15.2%	2.7%	-21%
	6	22.50	1.310	18.625		7.6%	22.2%	7.0%	-21%
scq	3	10.00	2.190	12.125		0.7%	5.8%	18.1%	18%

* (D-E) Evaluation of new covered call positions should be based on the asked price for the stock, the bid price for the option.

(G) Profit Expiration $= \dfrac{\text{Dividends} + \text{Lesser of the Stock Price or Strike}}{\text{Stock Price} - \text{Option Price}} - 1$

Calculations here do not allow for commissions but should in a real trading environment. If the call is in the money, subtract from the numerator commission (based on its tangible value) that would be incurred to repurchase the option at expiration. Add to the denominator commissions for purchasing the stock and selling the call.

(H) Profit to Expiration Annualized = $(G + 1)^{\wedge}(365/\text{Days to Expiration}) - 1$

Exhibit 11.4 Continued

(I) Loss Protection $= \dfrac{\text{Option Price}}{\text{Stock Price}}$

To allow for commissions, reduce the numerator by the commissions on purchase of the option and add to the denominator commissions to purchase the stock.

(J) Profit Protection $= 1 - \dfrac{\text{Strike Price}}{\text{Stock Price}}$

To allow for commissions, add to the denominator commissions to purchase the stock.

ROLLING: WHEN THE COVERED CALL HAS DONE ITS JOB

Rolling is a process of replacing an existing call with another that produces a covered call position with more favorable characteristics. It can be done any time prior to the expiration of the existing call, even just a few days after it was written or immediately before it expires. There are two reasons to roll: if much of the profit potential of the original position was realized or if much of the downside protection was used up. Rolling nails down the realized profit and restores the downside protection.

Once a covered call position is established, we monitor it in the same way as we evaluated the original position. Consider, for example, an at-the-money call written for $3 when the stock was $30. The profile of the original position looked like the one shown in Exhibit 11.5.

Exhibit 11.5 How Characteristics of a Covered Call Change Over Time

	Months to Expiration	Stock Price	Premium	Cost Basis	Annual Profit	Loss Protection	Profit
Initial Position	6	$30	$3.00	$27.00	22%	10%	0%
Later, it might look like either of these:							
Case #1:	1	$30	.38	29.62	17%	1%	0%
Case #2:	3	$35	5.50	29.50	7%	16%	14%
Case #3:	3	$25	.25	24.75	4%	1%	0%

The initial position offered an annualized return of more than 20% and a comfortable amount of loss protection. Later, in none of these three cases were both present. In Case #1, with one month to expiration, all but $0.38 of the original $3 call premium had been captured; the remaining $0.38 premium doesn't provide adequate loss protection. By rolling, we could nail down the profit. We might, for example, buy back the outstanding call for $0.38 pocketing a profit of $2.62. Simultaneously, we'd sell a new six-month call for $3, reestablishing a position with the same characteristics as the original.

In Case #2, with three months to run, the position still offered ample loss and profit protection, but with the stock up 5 points to $35, much of the original profit potential was realized. Now, we can buy back the outstanding call for $5.50 raising our investment in the position to $32.50. Since the stock is now $35, however, we've nailed down a profit of $2.50. Simultaneously, we'd sell a new six-month call struck at 35 for $3.50, reestablishing a position with the same characteristics as the original.

In Case #3, the stock slid 5 points. There's only 1% of loss protection left to cushion the position if the stock goes further south, and if it remains flat, the annualized return over the next three months would be only 4%. We'd buy back the call for $0.25, a gain of $2.75 on the call. We have a loss of $5 on the stock, however, so we have a net loss of $2.25 . . . which is less than half the loss we'd have suffered if we hadn't sold a call against the stock. Simultaneously, we'd sell a new six-month call struck at 25 for $2.50, reestablishing a position with the same characteristics as the original.

> Despite the thin downside protection and anemic return to expiration in Case #3, some investors would plan to retain the position, counting on a rebound in the stock to make up their loss. This optimistic view fails to give adequate consideration to risk, or the likelihood that they are no more likely to forecast the stock's rebound than they were able initially to forecast its decline.

CHOOSING THE NEW POSITION

The decision about whether to roll up (to a higher strike), down (to a lower strike), out (to a more distant expiration), or up and out, or down and out, is based on the characteristics you wish to reestablish. Often, certain calls will create far more attractive positions than others and it will be an easy choice. But there will be times that none are attractive.

In Exhibit 11.6, for example, we evaluated the rolling choices that might have been available to us for the position in Exhibit 11.5 described as Case #1.

Exhibit 11.6 Rolling Choices Available as of April 27

	Expiration	Strike	Bid	Ask	Dividend	Return to		Loss Protection	Profit
						Expiration	Annual		
Stock Price:									
Case #1*	May-93	$30.0	29.75	30.25					
			0.250	0.375	–	1%	17%	1%	0%
Difference between closing position now or at expiration: 21%									
Roll?	Jun-93	$30.0	0.625	XXXX	0.05	2%	17%	2%	0%
"	Jul-93	$25.0	5.250	XXXX	0.05	2%	11%	18%	16%
"	Jul-93	$30.0	1.000	XXXX	0.05	4%	18%	3%	0%
"	Aug-93	$30.0	2.250	XXXX	0.10	9%	30%	8%	0%

* Existing position.

Our existing position combines a short position in the May 30 call against a long position in the stock. With one month to expiration, that position no longer has adequate loss protection. The likely candidates for a roll are these calls: June 30, July 25 or 30, and August 30. We find that neither the June 30 or July 30 calls offer significantly more loss protection. The July 25 fills that bill and will deliver up the full 11% return even if the stock drops 16%, but its 11% annualized return is anemic. The August 30 call, however, offers an attractive combination of loss protection and annualized return. (*Note*: "Difference between closing position now or at expiration" is explained in the discussion of Exhibit 11.7.)

How alternate positions are evaluated. Although on occasion it's possible to buy below the "asked" price or sell above the "bid," normally we must buy at the "asked" price and sell at the "bid"—particularly when two sides to a transaction must be executed simultaneously, as is the case when establishing a covered call position or rolling. Thus, we evaluate new covered call positions by pricing the stock at the asked and the call at the bid. Similarly, a roll is evaluated by pricing the existing call (the call we must buy back) at the asked and the call that we might sell in its place at the bid. When we evaluate a roll, however, the stock is valued at the bid, the amount it would be worth to us if we went to sell it.

The *cost basis* of a new position is the bid price of the stock less the bid price of the call. (Thus, the cost basis of our existing covered call position, which combines the May 30 call and the stock, is $29.50, or $29.75–.25.) The *return to expiration* (assuming the stock remains unchanged) is equal to the dividends that will be received on the stock plus the lesser of the strike or the bid price of the stock divided by the cost basis of the position minus 1. (Here, it's $29.75/$29.50–1 = 1%.)

Commissions. Commissions are ignored in the previous examples but must be allowed in practice. The cost basis of a roll candidate should include the commission on the repurchase of the outstanding call as well as the sale of the new call. (By allowing for both commissions, the return offered by the roll candidate can be compared directly with the return offered by the existing position.)

When Not to Roll

In not all instances will you find a call worth rolling into. Consider what you would have done in Case #2 (Exhibit 11.5) if, when you went to roll, only the choices shown in Exhibit 11.7 were available.

Notice in Exhibit 11.7 that as of February, none of the available calls were attractive enough to roll into. The August 35 offered the best annualized return, 16%, but that was below our target, and the loss protection was meager compared to our existing position. Our choices, then, were (1) close out the position and open another from scratch, (2) hold, hoping that better opportunities to roll would arise in the weeks ahead, or (3) hold to expiration.

In fact, (2) and (3) offered far better prospects than first meet the eye. Notice that the difference between closing the position now or at expiration is 13%. (If we were to close out now, we'd receive $34.75 for the stock and pay $5.50 to buy back the call, netting $29.25. If allowed to expire, the stock would be called away: we'd receive $30 plus $0.05 dividends. The difference annualizes to 13%. If commissions were allowed for, the additional profits if held

Exhibit 11.7 Rolling Choices Available as of February 27

	Expiration	Strike	Bid	Ask	Dividend	Return to Expiration	Return to Annual	Loss Protection	Profit
Stock Price:			34.75	35.25					
Case #2*	May-93	$30.0	5.125	5.50	0.05	1%	7%	15%	14%

Annualized loss if closed now rather than at expiration: 13%

Roll?									
	May-93	$35.0	0.875	XXXX	0.05	3%	13%	3%	–1%
"	Aug-93	$30.0	6.000	XXXX	0.10	5%	10%	17%	14%
"	Aug-93	$35.0	2.250	XXXX	0.10	7%	16%	6%	–1%

* Existing position

to expiration would be even greater. For to close out now, we'd pay commissions on two trades—one to buy back the call, the second to sell the stock—but if the stock were called away, we'd pay commissions on only one trade—the sale of the stock.)

In all cases, of course, the decision of whether to roll, or which call to roll into, should also be based on the reward and risk characteristics of the position.

Placing Orders

How to place orders for covered calls and rolls is reviewed in Chapter 1, "The Basics." Placing orders for rolls is the equivalent of placing orders for spreads. Thus, an order to buy back an open June 30 call for $0.25 and sell the December 35 for $2 would be given as "Buy (to close) the June 30 XYZ call and sell (to open) the December 35 call for a net credit of $1.75." All option orders should, in addition, be contingent on the price of the stock. If the roll is at a debit, add "with the stock at this price or higher." If the roll is at a credit, add "with the stock at this price or lower."

SUMMING UP

Covered call writing is perhaps the most attractive of all investment strategies. Not only does it entail about half the risk of holding common stocks, providing substantial downside protection, but also it has generated returns which, on average, have exceeded those provided by common stocks. This is an attractive combination: reduced risk and comparable or better returns. Needless to say, however, not every position will perform as expected, so as in all investing, diversification is essential.

The options department of at least one major brokerage house has, at options seminars, encouraged institutional money managers to write covered calls indiscriminately, basing its recommendation on the assertion that over time, such a strategy would have worked to their advantage. No doubt, in its zeal it confused what would be of benefit to its customers with what would be of benefit to its own options desk. The first covered call funds did, indeed, compile excellent records, but by the mid-1980s a slew of covered call funds had sprung up and, in the following few years, the performance of the group as a whole slipped, probably because opportunities for selectivity diminished. While even during this period, adjusted for risk, their performance as a group was not unattractive, not all did well. *Value Line Options'* covered call recommendations continued to do well, however. Value Line's evaluation methods are proprietary, but the evaluation methods discussed in this book were developed since I left Value Line and, I believe, are likely to produce even better results. But investors who do not have the facilities to do the massive calculations necessary to screen all options, or to calculate the volatilities of the underlying stocks, may nevertheless find it convenient to turn to *Value Line Options* for estimated future volatilities and for broad screens of attractive covered call positions. Then, using the techniques described here, cull from those lists the issues likely to provide the best returns with the lowest risk.

HOW BEST TO USE *VALUE LINE OPTIONS*

Value Line Options determines the volatility of each stock by measuring the standard deviation of the stock's weekly price change over a five-year period. It then translates that volatility into "relative volatility" by comparing the stock's volatility to the median volatility of all 1,700 stocks it monitors. By assigning a relative volatility equal to "100%" to the median stock, it becomes easy to visualize the volatility, or risk, of any other investment. An investment with a relative volatility of 200%, for example, would be twice as risky as the median stock whereas another with a relative volatility of 50% would be half as risky as the median stock.

Relative volatility can be converted back into a volatility number by multiplying the volatility of the median stock by the relative volatility of the stock. Thus, if the volatility of the median stock was 35% and the stock's relative volatility was 50%, the stock's volatility would be 17.5%. Value Line's volatility calculations are updated quarterly, and at that time, it publishes the weekly standard deviation of the median stock over the previous five years. That weekly volatility figure can be converted to annual volatility by multiplying by the square root of 52.

All option pricing is based not on the underlying stock's historic volatility but on its estimated future volatility. As discussed in an earlier chapter, that estimate is arrived at by comparing the stock's historic volatility to its implied future volatility. While Value Line doesn't publish its estimate of the underlying stock's future volatility, its estimate can be derived from the relative volatility of the underlying stock and the relative volatility of the option, both of which it does publish, for while the relative volatility of the underlying stock is simply the historic volatility, *the relative volatility it shows for an option is based on its esti-mate of the stock's future volatility.* In essence, this figure is determined by multiplying its estimate of the stock's *future relative volatility* by the option's leverage. Thus, if the stock's future relative volatility was estimated to be 80% and the option was expected to move 10 times faster than the stock, the relative volatility of the option would be 800%.

Since both the relative volatility and leverage are pub-lished in *Value Line Options*, working backwards it is possi-ble to approximate Value Line's estimate of the stock's future volatility by dividing the option's relative volatility by its leverage.

Here's an example:

Option's relative volatility : 770%

Current Leverage	
+10%	**–10%**
+150	–70

This option's price is expected to rise 15 times faster than the common and fall 7 times faster. On average, then, it's expected to move 11 times faster than the common (15+7/2). Dividing the option's relative volatility, 770%, by 11, tells us that Value Line's estimate of the stock's *future relative volatility* was 70%.

Perform this calculation for several options on the stock. Most will fall within a small range. But as both lever-age and relative volatility figures are rounded, results from option to option will vary. The extent to which an option is over- or underpriced will also cause a variation, some-times rather wide for, as described in Chapter 9, the volatility of an option depends to a large extent on its initial price.

A comparison of the stock's estimated future volatility to its historic volatility provides an indication of the recent activity in the options on a given stock.

Covered Portfolio Writing: Covered Call Writing with a Twist

In which we learn of a variation of covered call writing you won't find in any books—a strategy which, at the expense of a bit more risk, expands both downside protection and upside potential.

No investment strategy, no matter how attractive, is without its disadvantages, and covered call writing is not an exception. In covered call writing:

1. You buy a stock because you expect it will rise in value, then sell a call against it in case it won't.

Thus you give up the upside potential of the stock beyond the strike of the call.

2. The downside protection of the position typically decreases over time. For example, if you sold a six-month call against your stock for $6, you begin with $6 of downside protection. Three months later that call might be worth $3, so you'd have just $3 of downside protection. One month after that it might be worth $2, then $1, then $0.50, etc. As the value of the call declines, so too does the downside protection.

3. When you go to write a call against your stock, you may not find one that's attractive to write.

ENTER "COVERED PORTFOLIO WRITING"

Covered portfolio writing is a strategy that, at the expense of a bit more risk, overcomes these disadvantages. Instead of writing calls against the stocks you own, the stocks you expect will perform best in the market during the period ahead, you sell the same dollar value of calls, but you write them against stocks you don't own, the stocks you expect will perform worst. (In effect, you construct a hedged portfolio: on one side you hold stocks long, on the other, naked calls short.) This does the following for you:

1. You give up none of the upside potential of your stocks.

2. The downside protection of the portfolio doesn't shrink. As the value of the short calls contracts, you simply write more to restore it to its original value. (Similarly, as the value of your stock portfolio rises, you may write more calls to maintain the same ratio of calls to stocks.)

3. You have complete freedom to search out and sell the most attractive calls on the least attractive stocks.

4. It's no longer necessary to buy back very low-priced, out-of-the-money calls in order to roll into others that offer more downside protection. You can let those calls expire worthless, saving commission and transaction costs, yet still maintain full downside protection.

5. As in covered call writing, there is no additional margin requirement. Your stocks provide all the margin you need. (In addition, as in covered writing, your portfolio of stocks—and your presence in the market—can be greater than your equity. If, for example, you invest $100,000 and sell calls worth $7,500, the $7,500 you take in may be invested in additional stocks, Treasuries or other income-bearing instruments.)

THE ADDED RISK

In a covered writing portfolio, any loss on one side is offset in part or in full by gains on the other. If the stock drops, the value of the calls must drop, too. In covered portfolio writing there is the added risk that you may lose on both sides: if you select poorly, the stocks could fall and the short calls rise.

Typically, however, even if your stock selections and call selections are no better than random, you would expect to do as well as you would writing covered calls—the gains and losses balancing out. In fact, since the odds favor the option writer, I found I added about 3% a year on average to the returns I might otherwise have earned from covered call writing. The added returns, however, came at the expense of added volatility: in some years, particularly when the market was tame, I added substantially to my returns; in others, particularly when the market moved markedly higher, my returns were cropped. Needless to say, if you have an effective system for "ranking" stocks, returns might have been greater than achieved with the aid of the Value Line ranking system.

POSTSCRIPT

A period in which covered portfolio writing performed particularly poorly for those who followed Value Line's recommendations occurred in early 1992. As would be expected, the performance of the Value Line equity funds, whose equity selections were dictated by the ranking system, was an embarrassment, too. By April 1992, a meeting was called to consider what action to take. The equity portfolio managers, tied irrevocably to a system that wasn't working, urged that they should be given greater discretion, noting that not only did the ranking system fail to discriminate during periods such as this when growth stocks were out of vogue, but that cyclical stocks, the stocks then leading the market, weren't its cup of tea at any time.

Sam Eisenstadt, however, who is credited with much of the development of the Value Line common stock ranking system and who has championed it against all criticism, argued that if his asset allocation model had been followed, the funds' performance would have been better. (Eisenstadt had developed a model to forecast the market three or four years earlier. Based on its forecasts, Eisenstadt recommended how much of the funds' portfolios should be invested in equities and how much in cash. As often happens, however, the model worked satisfactorily in back testing but never in practice. Eisenstadt, however, was convinced that in time the model would prove out. During this particular year, 1992, as was the case in 1991, the model was forecasting that the market would go lower and Eisenstadt was recommending that some 40% of the fund's portfolio be held in cash. As it happened, the market had risen about 30% in 1991 and had been trending higher in 1992, as well. None of this phased Eisenstadt.)

At last, however, one of the fund managers could be still no longer. "But Sam," he pointed out, "if we followed your model last year when the market rose 30%, our fund performance would have suffered even more."

"Yeah," Sam replied, "but with less money in stocks, you'd have had less volatility."

"You mean," asked the fund manager, "we'd have made less money but would have been happier about it?"

Hedging the Market: How to Win at Options without Calling the Market

This is the second of the two option strategies likely to pay off consistently. Unlike covered call writing and covered portfolio writing, which are low in risk, this is a strategy for investors willing to accept much higher risk to tap the really huge profits options can generate. It is another strategy you won't find in other books. Based on published recommendations, a similar strategy has been profitable, on average, each year since first recommended in 1980. Over this entire span, it has generated indicated compound average annual returns in excess of 70% a year.

THE SINGLE BIGGEST PROBLEM OPTION INVESTORS FACE

Since most stocks move with the market, no matter how cheaply you buy an option or how rich the price for which you sell it, if the market goes against you, you can expect to lose a good chunk of your investment, and perhaps all. Indeed, even if you were able to buy a call worth $5 for just a few pennies, if the market tanked and the call expired out of the money, your investment would be wiped out. So if your option strategy is sensitive to market movement and you continually reinvest whatever profits you realize, eventually the market will sabotage you and you'll wind up losing most or all of your stake.

HEDGING

The obvious answer to this dilemma is to search for an option strategy that makes money regardless of which way the market goes. One strategy that many brokers and textbooks recommend is spreading. Unfortunately, spreads don't fill the bill. For a spread to be profitable, the market must move in your favor. If it doesn't, your investment is wiped out, as can be seen in Exhibit 13.1.

The particular spread in Exhibit 13.1 is profitable if the stock rises above $31.88. Commissions are not taken into account here, however; if they were, the stock would have to rise even further for the spread to pay off. A spread, then, won't protect you against an adverse market move.

Exhibit 13.1   Profile of a Bull Call Spread

	Strike	Price				
Buy Call	$30	$2.98				
Sell Call	35	1.10				
Net Cost		**$1.88**				
Stock at Expiration:	$25.00	$30.00	$31.88	$32.50	$35.00	$40.00
Value of Long Call:	0	0	1.88	2.50	5.00	10.00
Value of Short Call:	0	0	0	0	0	(5.00)
Value of Spread at						
Expiration:	0	0	$ 1.88	$ 2.50	$ 5.00	$ 5.00
Net Debit:	1.88	1.88	1.88	1.88	1.88	1.88
Profit (Loss)*:	($1.88)	($1.88)	$ —	$0.62	$ 3.12	$3.12

* Before commissions.

WHY SPREADERS MUST LOSE IF THEY CAN'T CALL THE MARKET

Up until now, we have evaluated spreads as we did in Exhibit 13.1, that is, by focusing on the range of prices over which the spread would or would not be profitable. In a sense, this method of analysis implies that with this knowledge, we can make an informed estimate of whether the hedge will be a viable investment. In other words, if we are able to predict whether the stock will move into a particular price range. Those with this talent have, no doubt, already become rich. Others, not so fortunate, can evaluate spreads based on the log-normal price distribution of the underlying stock in the way we evaluate options (see Chapter 10). That is, with the guidance of the log-normal distribution, we can determine the probable occurrence of various prices at the time the options expire and combine that projection with the profit or loss the spread would generate at each price. That would provide an estimate of the profitability of the hedge. A Lotus worksheet that will do just that can be found in Appendix 13-A at the end of this chapter. It is similar to the worksheet in Chapter 10 with the exception that in evaluating a spread, we are determining the profit or loss of two (or more) options instead of just one.

With the help of this worksheet, you can find the amount you can afford to pay for a bull spread or the credit you'd want to receive for a bear spread to earn an adequate risk-adjusted return on your investment. Exhibit 13.2 shows an example.

Exhibit 13.2 An Evaluation of a Spread

Stock	Price: $35	Dividend: None	Relative volatility: 100%

Spread: Number of Days to expiration: 120

	Bull Spread	Bear Spread
Long Call Struck at:	$35	$40
Short Call Struck at:	$40	$35
Relative Volatility of Spread:	615%	235%
Indicated	Debit $1.66	Credit $2.42
Estimated Value at Expiration:	$1.99	$1.99
Profit:	$ .33	$ .43
Investment:	$1.66	$5.00 – $2.42 (margin less credit)
Return on Investment:	20%	16.4%

The returns on investment shown in Exhibit 13.2 are before commissions. In Chapter 7, I asserted that spreads offer very little chance of profit even if commissions are ignored, and that after commissions, the most likely outcome is a loss equal to the cost of commissions. Why this is so will now become clear.

If you were to set up this bull spread at the "fair" value of these options, it would cost you $1.99, the expected value of these options at expiration. That makes the expected profit on the spread zero. Add in commissions and it's a loss.

To make a profit on this spread, you'd have to buy the long option below its fair value and/or sell the short option above its fair value.

There are indeed mispriced options around. But here's the rub: prices of options on the same stock tend to rise and fall together. If you succeed in finding an underpriced option to buy, you'd probably have to sell the other at a discount. Any saving on one is likely to be offset by the loss on the other, so in the end, you'd probably be unable to buy the spread below its "fair" price or sell it above its "fair" price. Thus, if you can't call the market, over time the best you can hope for is to break even—even if you don't pay commissions.

Even assuming that you could find mispriced options so that these spreads could be set up at the desired debit or credit, as suggested in Chapter 7, once commissions are taken in account, the odds badly tilt against you. The worksheet in Appendix 13.A allows for commissions at rates you choose. Run the spreads in Exhibit 13.2 through the worksheet at the lowest commission rates discount brokers charge and you will find that after commissions, the return on the bull spread skids from 20% to 9% and the return on the bear spread slides similarly.

HOW TO TRADE OPTIONS WITHOUT THE NEED TO CALL THE MARKET

What if you could set up a hedged option position on a stock not at the "fair" prices of the options, but at the prices indicated by our model? For example, in Chapter 10 we found that a 120-day call struck at 30 on a $30 stock of average risk would be worth $2.96 at expiration . . . and that to earn a fair return on that call, we'd want to buy it for $2.33 or sell it for $4.01.

Obviously we couldn't buy a call on a stock at $2.33 and simultaneously sell another on the same stock for $4.01, but what if we could find two different stocks, both priced at $30, both of average risk, and we were able to sell calls on one for $4.01 and buy calls on the other for $2.33?

If those two stocks moved with the market, we'd have a locked-in profit. The two option positions would offset each other; whether the stocks went up or down, the gain on one would exactly equal the loss on the other, so we'd be certain to pocket $1.68, the difference in price between the two, as shown in Exhibit 13.3.

In combination, these two positions would provide a perfect hedge against the market. We'd pocket a profit of $1.68 regardless of whether the market rose or fell. Moreover, the risk would be relatively small—about one-quarter the risk normal in trading naked options.

If this hedge could only be established if we could find identical pairs of stocks, one with overpriced calls and the other with underpriced calls, it would be difficult, indeed,

Exhibit 13.3   Hedged Option Positions

Stock at Expiration:	$25.00	$30.00	$35.00	$40.00
Value of Long Call:	0	0	5.00	10.00
Value of Short Call:	0	0	−5.00	−10.00
Value of Spread at Expiration:	$0	$0	$0	$0
Net Credit:	$1.68	$1.68	$1.68	$1.68
Profit (Loss)*:	$1.68	$1.68	$1.68	$1.68

* Before commissions.

to set up. But that's not necessary. We can accomplish the same objective by buying underpriced calls for one side of the hedge and selling overpriced calls for the other. (For example, if we bought two 120-day calls on the $30 stock for $2.33 each, instead of selling two 120-day calls on a $30 stock for $4.01, we could sell one 120-day call on a $60 stock for $8.02).

CAN SUCH A HEDGE ACTUALLY BE SUCCESSFUL?

I first recommended such hedges in 1980. Since then, based on options actually recommended for purchase and sale in *Value Line Options*, the hedge generated estimated average annual profits in excess of 70% a year, this despite the fact that the hedge was tied into the Value Line ranking system and so failed during periods when the Value Line ranking system failed. There are, however, certain advantages to be gained in managing this hedge without their ranking system.[1]

HOW TO SET UP THE HEDGE

For this hedge to be successful, there must be equal exposure on both sides of the hedge. Experience has shown that puts are relatively inactive: rarely will you find a large enough assortment to provide the desired diversification. In addition, oddly, put and call premiums don't always move together. Best results, therefore, are likely to be achieved by setting up the hedge with long calls on one side and short calls on the other, as follows:

1. The "fair" value of the options on the two sides of the hedge should be approximately equal. The "fair" value is the expected value of the options, as deter-

---

[1] The Value Line option ranking system ranks options for buying or selling based in part on the under- or overvaluation of the option and in part on the expected performance of the underlying stock. Options that are top-ranked for buying may be underpriced or may simply be on stocks that are top-ranked for performance. Options top-ranked for selling may be underpriced or may be simply on stocks ranked worst for buying (hence considered best for selling). *Value Line Options* subscribers are advised to set up the long call/short call hedge by buying top-ranked calls and selling bottom-ranked calls. Their hedge performance, then, has been about half based on the stock ranks and about half on the under- or overvaluation of the options. Since the Value Line common stock ranking system has performed poorly over this time period, the returns generated by the hedge are likely to be a result of the system's ability to identify under- and overpriced options. Setting up this hedge ex the ranking system—that is, strictly on the basis of the under- or overvaluation of the options—would be likely to yield even better results.

mined by the stock's log-normal distribution or, similarly, the Black-Scholes model.

2. The dollar value of the option premiums on the two sides of the hedge will not be equal.

   Referring again to Chapter 10, recall that we found a 120-day call struck at 30 would be worth $2.96 at expiration. To earn a fair return on that call, we would want to buy it for $2.33 or sell it at $4.01. If we found two complementary options and we set up a hedge by buying one at $2.33 and selling the other at $4.01, the "fair" value of the options on each side would be an identical $2.96, but the premium on the long side would be $2.33 while the premium on the short side would be $4.01.

3. The capital committed on each side of the hedge will also be different.

   To buy that option for $2.33, we'd lay out just that amount. To sell the other for $4.01, we'd lay out $6 for margin (the stock was $30). Generally, you'll find that about three times as much money is committed on the short side of the hedge as the long side.

4. For the hedge to be balanced, the risk on both sides of the hedge should be reasonably equal. This means that the relative volatility of options on both sides of the hedge should be reasonably comparable.

If possible, the relative volatilities of the stocks on both sides should be reasonably comparable, too.

Select a range of relative volatilities with which you're comfortable (such as from 800% to 1,200% for options) and select positions for the hedge within that range.

In Chapter 10 it was pointed out that the risk or relative volatility in an option "position" is different from the risk in the option itself. The risk in the option "position" depends, in part, on the amount paid for the option (or the margin that must be posted to sell it). The object is to balance the risk in the options, not the option "positions," so base selections, whether for the long or short side of the hedge, on the intrinsic risk in the option at its "fair" value (rather than at the price paid for it).

HOW TO DIVERSIFY

For this hedge to work, diversification is a must. The object is to have a sufficiently diversified portfolio on both sides so that each side is likely to move with the market. To accomplish this, you should:

1. Hold options on at least 10 companies (15 or more would be better) on each side of the hedge.

   The size of each position should be large enough to keep commission costs within reasonable bounds; in no case should commissions exceed 5%. Usually, for retail accounts, this requires that the initial premium value of each option position should be at least $1,000. A hedge with 15 options on each side, then, would require a minimum cash outlay of about $60,000, $15,000 on the long side and $45,000 on the short side for margin. A reserve of another $15,000 or so—in the event that additional margin may later be required—would be prudent, as well.

2. Initially, the size of each long position should be about equal. The size of short positions should be about equal, too, but short premiums will be larger than long premiums, so short positions will be larger than long positions.

3. Options on the long side should be on stocks in different, unrelated industries.

4. Options on stocks on the short side should also be on stocks in different, unrelated industries, but if possible on the same industries as the options on the long side.

5. Stagger expiration dates on both sides of the hedge.

RISK

In a hedge of this sort, the object is for the stocks on each side to move in line with the market. If we achieve that, the stock movement on one side offsets the stock movement on the other and, as illustrated in Exhibit 13.3, we pocket the original credit. Is this likely to happen? The broader our diversification, the more likely it is that the two sides will do so. But if they don't, there are only two other possibilities: (a) the stocks on the long call side can rise while the stocks on the short side fall; or (b) the stocks on the long side can fall while those on the short side rise. Exhibit 13.4 examines what might happen in those cases. In Exhibit 13.4a, where the stocks underlying the long calls rise while those underlying the short calls fall, the profit on the hedge would be huge; in Exhibit 13.4b, where the stocks move oppositely, the hedge would suffer a large loss, though part would be offset by the original credit.

Exhibit 13.4a When Stocks Don't Move Together

Stock at Expiration:	$35.00	$40.00
Value of Long Call:	5.00	10.00
Stock at Expiration:	$25.00	$30.00
Value of Short Call:	.00	.00
Value of Spread at Expiration:	**$ 5.00**	**$10.00**
Original Credit:	$1.68	$1.68
Profit (Loss)*:	**$6.68**	**$11.68**

* Before commissions.

Exhibit 13.4b When Stocks Don't Move Together

Stock at Expiration:	$25.00	$30.00
Value of Long Call:	.00	.00
Stock at Expiration:	$35.00	$40.00
Value of Short Call:	–5.00	–10.00
Value of Spread at Expiration:	$–5.00	$–10.00
Original Credit:	$1.68	$1.68
Profit (Loss)*:	$–3.32	$–8.32

* Before commissions.

Thus, this hedge is not risk-free. Broad diversification can reduce the risk, but it cannot eliminate it.

Statistics suggest that approximately 30% of stock price movement is market-related and 70% caused by events specific to the company or its industry. By diversifying, we can reduce company-related risk, the events in one company or industry offsetting events in another. If we held enough different stocks, we could eliminate company-related risk entirely. To do that, however, we'd have to hold virtually all stocks . . . thus we'd essentially be holding the "market." Surprisingly, though, studies indicate we can diversify away a large percentage of company-related risk by holding just 10 to 15 unrelated stocks. Exhibit 13.5 is an estimate of the extent to which a properly diversified portfolio decreases company-related risk.

Exhibit 13.5 How Diversification Reduces Risk

Number of Issues	Percentage of Total Risk	Percentage Total Risk is Reduced	Percentage Company-Related Risk Is Reduced
1	100%	0%	0%
2	80%	20%	29%
3	75%	25%	36%
4	70%	30%	43%
5	65%	35%	50%
10	50%	50%	71%
20	45%	55%	79%
40	40%	60%	86%
100	35%	65%	93%
2,000	30%	70%	100%

To understand how effectively diversification improves a hedged position by reducing risk, consider the simplest hedge in which you bought just one call on one side of the hedge and sold one call on the other side. Exhibit 13.6 assumes the calls were the same ones discussed in Exhibit 13.5.

There are no surprises in these figures. Over the 12 years that this hedge has been recommended, the average annual return on investment was 74%. What may be surprising, however, is how low the relative volatility (risk) of this hedge becomes when the two sides are properly diversified. Exhibit 13.5 shows that by holding 10 unrelated positions on each side, company-related risk is reduced by 71%. Thus, with 10 diversified positions on each side, the relative volatility of this hedge drops to about 190%. (Bear in mind,

Exhibit 13.6   A Two-Option Perfect "Hedge"

	Long Call	Short Call	Combined Position
Stock Price	$30	$30	
Strike	$30	$30	
Days to Expiration	120	120	
Relative Volatility	872%	379%	626%
Estimated Value at Expiration	$2.96	$2.96	
Buy (Sell) at	$2.33	$4.01	
Expected Profit	$ .63	$1.05	$1.68
Invested Capital	$2.33	$6.00 (margin)	$8.33
Return on Investment			20%
Annualized Return on Investment			74%

however, that a diversified 10-position stock portfolio would have a relative volatility of about 50% if each stock had a relative volatility of 100%.)

Is risk really this low? Probably not. In practice, it is extremely difficult today to assemble a portfolio of 10 companies whose product lines do not overlap to some extent. In addition, over time, the size and relative volatilities of the positions in the hedge shift, gradually reducing the diversification. Consequently, in practice, the relative volatility of this hedge may be closer to 250%, or five times the risk in a stock portfolio. Still, the hedge would have a reward/risk ratio of about 0.30 (74%/250%), clearly attractive.

MAINTAINING THE HEDGE

The object in managing the hedge is (1) to retain, within reason, the original balance between the two sides and (2) to retain the diversification between positions. To do so, it is necessary to trim back positions that balloon so the performance of the hedge doesn't hang on one or a few positions, and close out positions whose relative volatility has changed sharply. In addition, (3) it's advantageous to cash out positions that become substantially mispriced.

1. *Balance.* Over time, if one side of the hedge becomes larger than the other, the protection the hedge affords against an adverse move in the market is reduced. This can be corrected by reinvesting funds that are freed up as positions are closed in the "light" side of the hedge.

2. *Diversification.* The diversification within the hedge is eroded when positions jump in value relative to others or if a wide change occurs in the relative volatility of a position. A position that shrinks in value is no problem; two or more such positions can be considered the equivalent of a full-sized position. But when a position doubles in size relative to others, it exerts twice the clout, and if it triples, it's the equivalent of three positions. When that happens because the underlying stock has taken off, the temptation is to let it run. At what point variant positions should be cut back depends partly on the added risk you will accept, the time to expiration, and commissions.

3. *Cashing Out*. If option premiums shift dramatically, it may be worth taking profits. When a call bought when it was underpriced becomes so overpriced that you'd be happy to sell it, or an overpriced call you sold becomes so underpriced that it's worth buying, cash them out if it pays to do so after commissions.

CAN *VALUE LINE OPTIONS* HELP?

The instructions for managing the hedge given here are, of course, not quite the same as those given to Value Line subscribers. That's because Value Line's option ranking system will select calls for buying if the underlying stock is ranked favorably—even if the calls are not underpriced. Similarly, a call recommended for selling may not have been overpriced but simply on a stock ranked unfavorably. Thus, for an option hedge based on those recommendations to be fully successful, the common stock ranking system must discriminate successfully, something it hasn't done, on balance, over the past 10 years. It seems likely, then, that if Value Line's option recommendations had been based entirely on the under- and overvaluation of the options (rather in part on the ranks of the underlying stocks), the hedge results would have been even better.

Also bear in mind that in Value Line's ranking system, stocks in the same or related industries tend to rise and fall in rank together. The best hedge, however, is constructed by buying underpriced calls and offsetting them against overpriced calls on stocks in the same industries—a combination rarely found in Value Line's option recommendations.

APPENDIX 13.A
Lotus Spreadsheet for a Call Bull Spread
(Cell formulas at end)

1	BULL CALL SPREADS: Evaluation Based on "Negative" Risk							
2	# Days: 100		Strike	Price	Stock Div'd:		$1.00	(to opt expire)
3	Long Options:		$30.00	$4.00	Rel. Vol'y:		100%	
4	Short Options:		$35.00	$1.00	Price:		$35.00	
5	Cost of Spread:			$3.12	Desired ROI:		12.0%	
6	Suggested Cost:			$3.14	Commission			
7	Difference:			($0.02)	Discount:		0%	
8	Est'd Value of Spread:			$3.34				

	A	B	C	D	E	F	G	H	I
9									
10			Negative risk		Lever-	Rel	Desired ROI			
11			($)	(%)	age	Vol'y	for			
12	Stock	$2.01	5.7%		100%	Period			
13	Spread	$0.38	12.3%	2.14	214%	6.5%			
14									
15				Tangible		Commis-			
16	Stock	Stock		Value of		sion		Value of Spread		Prob-
17	Incre-	Wt'd		Option		to		Weigh-	Cumu-	abil-
18	ment	Value	Long	Short	Close	($)	ted	lative	ity
19	−33.83	0.00	0.00	0.00	0	0.00	0.00	0.00	0.0%
20	−32.67	0.00	0.00	0.00	0	0.00	0.00	0.00	0.0%
	...	...	...	...	...	...	...	...	...
79	36.17	0.00	41.17	36.17	0.262	4.74	0.00	3.34	0.0%
80	37.33	0.00	42.33	37.33	0.262	4.74	0.00	3.34	0.0%

B2:	Insert: # Days
D3:	Insert: Strike price of long calls
E3:	Insert: Long call premium
H3:	Insert: Stock's relative volatility
D4:	Insert: Strike of short call
E4:	Insert: Short call premium
H4:	Insert: Stock price
E5:	+E3-E4+(@VLOOKUP(E3,K7..L19,1)+@VLOOKUP(E4,K7..L19,1))*(1-H7)

H5:   Insert: Desired annual ROI on stock with 100% relative volatility

E6:   +E8/(1+F13)

E7:   +E5-E6

A commission lookup table should be installed in K7..L19 with the maximum commission rate applicable, as follows:

Line	K Option Price	L Commission Per Share (Full Rate)
7	$0.00	$0.00
8	$0.25	$0.02
9	$0.50	$0.03
	. . .	. . .
19	$50.00	$0.50

H7:   Insert: Discount from maximum commission rate you will receive on this trade

E8:   +H80

B12:   +B50-T50*H2

C12:   +B12/H4

E12:   +H3

B13:   @ @VLOOKUP($E$5,F19..T82,14)*E5+(@VLOOKUP(0,F19..H80,2)-@VLOOKUP(E5,F19..H80,2))

C13:   +B13/$E$5

D13:   +C13/$C$12

E13:   +$H$3*D13

F13:   +($H$5*E13+1)^($B$2/365)-1

A19:   Insert: Difference in stock price from $H$4

B19:   +A19*I19

C19:   @IF(O21$D$3,O21-$D$3,0)

D19:   @IF(O21$D$4,O21-$D$4,0)

E19:   (@VLOOKUP(C19,$K$7..$L$18,1)+@VLOOKUP(D19,$K$7..$L$18,1))*(1 -$H$7)

F19:   +C19-D19-E19

G19:   +F19*I19

H19:   +G19

I19:   Insert: Probability from log-normal distribution

A20:   Insert: Difference in stock price from $H$4

B20:   +A20*I20

C20: @IF(O22$D$3,O22-$D$3,0)
D20: @IF(O22$D$4,O22-$D$4,0)
E20: (@VLOOKUP(C20,$K$7..$L$18,1)+@VLOOKUP(D20,$K$7..$L$18,1))*(1 -$H$7)
F20: +C20-D20-E20
G20: +F20*I20
H20: +H19+G20
I20: Insert: Probability from log-normal distribution

Copy all cell formulas down to line 80 (or lower, if desired).

APPENDIX 13.B
Lotus Spreadsheet for a Call Bear Spread

BEAR CALL SPREADS: Evaluation Based on "Negative" Risk

Change these cells in the Bull Spread worksheet:
E6: +E8-H8*F13
E8: -H80
F8: Margin:
H8: Insert: margin per share to establish spread
B12: +B80-B50+(1-T50)*H2
B13: +H80-@VLOOKUP(-E5,F19..H80,2)+(1-@VLOOKUP(-E5,F19..T80,14))*E5
C13: +B13/-$E$5

Writing Low-Priced
Naked Options

In which we discover that if your object is to sell over-priced options, the place to dig for them is in low-priced neighborhoods . . . that if you must select blindfolded (heaven forbid), write low-priced, out-of-the-money calls on low-priced stocks . . . for ever-optimistic, investors overpay for "cheap" options, taking the short odds in the hope of a big payoff . . . and so sellers, who know what they're about and who diversify adequately to spread their risk, in time typically make out like bandits.

How do you spot a good deal? To evaluate a proposition put to the company in 1991 by representatives of Kansas

City's Board of Trade, Value Line's Chairwoman listed the pros and cons, a time-honored formula. "Let's list the reasons why we wouldn't want to go into this venture and why we would," she began. "Let's begin with the reasons not to. First, we could lose our entire business. Now what's a second reason against?"

In the world of options, a question that often comes up is how can it pay to write low-priced naked options, options selling for a sixteenth, an eighth, or a quarter, particularly since margin requirements are such that a writer must often put up as much money to write a $0.06 call as to write one for $5? Indeed, suppose, for example, you had the choice of writing two calls on a $15 stock, one a six-month call struck at $12.50 selling for $3 and the other a one-month call struck at $17.50 for $0.25. Out-of-pocket margin requirements for the first are $3, for the second $1.50. Which should you write?

Of course, the first thing you'd do is look at the likely value of those calls at expiration and their inherent risk. If this stock were of average volatility, here's what you'd find:

	Strike	Expected Value at Expiration	Relative Volatility	Profit	ROI	Annualized ROI
Six-month call	$12.50	$3.15	415%	−$0.15	− 5%	−10%
Six-month call	17.50	.05	320%	+.20	+13%	+350%

The choice seems clear. The lower-priced call was overpriced, less risky, and was likely to produce a whopping return whereas the higher-priced call was underpriced and likely to produce a loss.

But what if the stock cooperated by going south? In that case, you'd pocket the entire $3 premium from the higher-priced call but just $0.25 from the other. Would you then be better off selling the higher priced call? Let's see:

	Strike	Expected Value at Expiration	Relative Volatility	Profit	ROI	Annualized ROI
Six-month call	$12.50	$.00	415%	+3.00	+100%	+300%
One-month call	17.50	.00	320%	+.25	+17%	+536%

Even under this assumption, the annualized return from the lower-priced call is far superior. Yet, while the answer seems clear cut, it's not quite this easy. Risk in out-of-the-money options tends to rise rapidly as expiration approaches. Furthermore, a $1 change in the price of a stock will produce a much larger change, percentage-wise, in the price of a low-priced, out-of-the-money option than in a higher-priced, in-the-money option. In addition, commissions take a heftier bite out of lower-priced options than higher-priced ones.

Since the potential payoff in a low-priced option is many, many times the original price of the option—as in lotteries, investors appear willing to overpay and accept unfavorable odds in the hopes of winning a huge payoff. Thus, although the option writer must "win" several times for each "loss" simply to break even, the odds typically favor the option writer. It follows, then, that the place to find these overpriced opportunities is in near-to-expiration and out-of-the money options, particularly those on low-priced stocks.

HOW MUCH MARGIN?

Does it pay to write a short-term, out-of-the-money option at $0.50? at $0.25? at $0.125? or at $0.625? Assuming the option expires worthless, the answer, of course, depends on the return you wish to earn, the amount of the margin requirement, and the term of the option. Exhibit 14.1 provides an easy-to-use guide to determine out-of-pocket margin requirements (before commissions):

Exhibit 14.1 Out-of-Pocket Margin Requirement for Writing Calls (Excludes Option Premium)

			Percentage Option Is Out of the Money								
	-30%	-25%	-20%	-15%	-10%	-9%	-8%	-7%	-6%	-5%	
Strike $10	$0.70	0.75	0.80	0.85	.90	.92	1.04	1.16	1.28	1.40	
			Percentage Option Is Out of><In the Money								
	-4%	-3%	-2%	-1%	0%	5%	10%	15%	20%		
Strike $10	$1.52	1.64	1.76	1.88	2.00	2.10	2.20	2.30	2.40		

In Exhibit 14.1, notice that at –10%, indicating that the option is 10% out of the money (i.e., the stock is $9), the margin requirement is $0.90 a share. At +10%, indicating the option is 10% in the money (i.e., the stock is $11), the margin requirement is $2.20 a share. At 0%, indicating the option is at the money (i.e., the stock is $10), the margin requirement is $2. Margin requirements are proportional to the strike, so the exhibit may be used to quickly calculate margin requirements at all prices. For example, the out-of-pocket margin requirement for an option struck at $50, which is 4% out of the money (i.e., the stock's at $48) would be $7.60 ($50/$10 × $1.52).

AT WHAT MINIMUM PRICE IS AN OPTION ATTRACTIVE TO WRITE?

Now that we know how much margin we have to post, it's a simple matter to calculate the size of the option premium that will provide an acceptable return if a short-term option expires worthless. Exhibit 14.2a shows, for example, that you can earn a 50% return on a margin outlay of $2 on an option four weeks from expiration selling for just $0.06 after commissions. Similarly, on a margin outlay of $4, you'll earn a 50% annual return on an option expiring in four weeks selling for $0.13, but to earn 75% (Exhibit 14.2b), with that same margin outlay, the option must sell for $0.18, and for a 100% return (Exhibit 14.2c), it must bring in $0.22.

FINAL NOTES

If there is only a choice between buying or writing options, the advantage is always with the writer. Still, though writing short-term, low-priced, out-of-the-money options can be highly profitable, the risk of stock prices taking a sudden move against you means the risk is high. Diversification, then, in terms of the underlying stocks and months of expiration, is a must. The decision of whether to write such options must take commissions into account, too, for they can be high, percentage-wise, in low-priced options.

Exhibit 14.2a Option Price That Will Provide an Annual Return of 50% (if option expires worthless)

Weeks to Expira-tion	Margin Requirement										
	$1	$2	$3	$4	$5	$6	$7	$8	$9	$10	$11
1	0.01	0.02	0.02	0.03	0.04	0.05	0.05	0.06	0.07	0.08	0.09
2	0.02	0.03	0.05	0.06	0.08	0.09	0.11	0.13	0.14	0.16	0.17
3	0.02	0.05	0.07	0.09	0.12	0.14	0.17	0.19	0.21	0.24	0.26
4	0.03	0.06	0.10	0.13	0.16	0.19	0.22	0.25	0.29	0.32	0.35
5	0.04	0.08	0.12	0.16	0.20	0.24	0.28	0.32	0.36	0.40	0.44
6	0.05	0.10	0.14	0.19	0.24	0.29	0.34	0.38	0.43	0.48	0.53
7	0.06	0.11	0.17	0.22	0.28	0.34	0.39	0.45	0.50	0.56	0.62
8	0.06	0.13	0.19	0.26	0.32	0.39	0.45	0.51	0.58	0.64	0.71
9	0.07	0.15	0.22	0.29	0.36	0.44	0.51	0.58	0.65	0.73	0.80
10	0.08	0.16	0.24	0.32	0.41	0.49	0.57	0.65	0.73	0.81	0.89
11	0.09	0.18	0.27	0.36	0.45	0.54	0.63	0.72	0.81	0.90	0.99
12	0.10	0.20	0.29	0.39	0.49	0.59	0.69	0.78	0.88	0.98	1.08

Exhibit 14.2b Option Price That Will Provide an Annual Return of 75% (if option expires worthless)

Weeks to Expira-tion	Margin Requirement										
	$1	$2	$3	$4	$5	$6	$7	$8	$9	$10	$11
1	0.01	0.02	0.03	0.04	0.05	0.06	0.08	0.09	0.10	0.11	0.12
2	0.02	0.04	0.07	0.09	0.11	0.13	0.15	0.17	0.20	0.22	0.24
3	0.03	0.07	0.10	0.13	0.16	0.20	0.23	0.26	0.30	0.33	0.36
4	0.04	0.09	0.13	0.18	0.22	0.26	0.31	0.35	0.40	0.44	0.48
5	0.06	0.11	0.17	0.22	0.28	0.33	0.39	0.44	0.50	0.55	0.61
6	0.07	0.13	0.20	0.27	0.33	0.40	0.47	0.53	0.60	0.67	0.73
7	0.08	0.16	0.23	0.31	0.39	0.47	0.55	0.63	0.70	0.78	0.86
8	0.09	0.18	0.27	0.36	0.45	0.54	0.63	0.72	0.81	0.90	0.99
9	0.10	0.20	0.31	0.41	0.51	0.61	0.71	0.81	0.92	1.02	1.12
10	0.11	0.23	0.34	0.45	0.57	0.68	0.80	0.91	1.02	1.14	1.25
11	0.13	0.25	0.38	0.50	0.63	0.75	0.88	1.01	1.13	1.26	1.38
12	0.14	0.28	0.41	0.55	0.69	0.83	0.96	1.10	1.24	1.38	1.52

Exhibit 14.2c Option Price That Will Provide an Annual Return of 100% (if option expires worthless)

Weeks to Expira-tion	Margin Requirement										
	$1	$2	$3	$4	$5	$6	$7	$8	$9	$10	$11
1	0.01	0.03	0.04	0.05	0.07	0.08	0.09	0.11	0.12	0.13	0.15
2	0.03	0.05	0.08	0.11	0.14	0.16	0.19	0.22	0.24	0.27	0.30
3	0.04	0.08	0.12	0.16	0.20	0.24	0.29	0.33	0.37	0.41	0.45
4	0.05	0.11	0.16	0.22	0.27	0.33	0.38	0.44	0.49	0.55	0.60
5	0.07	0.14	0.21	0.28	0.34	0.41	0.48	0.55	0.62	0.69	0.76
6	0.08	0.17	0.25	0.33	0.42	0.50	0.58	0.67	0.75	0.83	0.92
7	0.10	0.20	0.29	0.39	0.49	0.59	0.68	0.78	0.88	0.98	1.08
8	0.11	0.23	0.34	0.45	0.56	0.68	0.79	0.90	1.01	1.13	1.24
9	0.13	0.25	0.38	0.51	0.64	0.76	0.89	1.02	1.15	1.27	1.40
10	0.14	0.29	0.43	0.57	0.71	0.86	1.00	1.14	1.28	1.43	1.57
11	0.16	0.32	0.47	0.63	0.79	0.95	1.11	1.26	1.42	1.58	1.74
12	0.17	0.35	0.52	0.69	0.87	1.04	1.21	1.39	1.56	1.73	1.91

PORTFOLIO MANAGEMENT

Portfolio Management, Risk, and Diversification

It is here that we put it all together—how to construct a portfolio that targets an acceptable level of risk; how to diversify properly in order to put the odds to work for you; and under what conditions positions should be closed out or replaced.

WHY DIVERSIFY?

Most investors think of risk only in terms of a rise or fall in the market or a company's fortunes. But risk is a function of leverage, as well, and leverage can have a greater impact. There are three sources of leverage: (1) the leverage inherent in the security itself, (2) the security's leverage as it is altered by financial leverage, and (3) the portfolio's leverage or risk as it is altered by diversification.

SECURITY-RELATED LEVERAGE

Leverage is a characteristic of an investment position. One option might pay off 1-to-1; risk $1 to make $1. Another might pay off 7-to-1. It is seven times as risky; risk $1 to make $7. If these were even money bets, in the first you'd expect to win once and lose once in two chances. In the second, you'd expect to win once and lose six times in seven chances.

POSITION-RELATED LEVERAGE

The leverage of an investment position is also a function of the financial position. If you buy on 50% margin, your leverage or risk is doubled. If you put up twice as much capital, you have one-half the leverage so one-half the risk. When you sell naked options, you normally must put up three times as much capital so you have just one-third the risk inherent in the option itself.

> (*Note*: One strategy advocated for reducing risk is the so-called "90-10" strategy. The bulk of the capital is invested in T-bills or something about as safe. Only the interest earned is put at risk. For example, if T-bills payed 10%, with an initial $1,000 you'd buy $910 of T-bills and $90 of options. By the end of the year, after interest, your T-bills would be worth $1,000, so even if your options got wiped out, your original capital would

be preserved. What you did was deleverage your portfolio drastically. This strategy has a number of drawbacks, not the least of which is that only a fraction of the portfolio is actively invested.)

PORTFOLIO-RELATED LEVERAGE

As positions are added to a portfolio, the leverage (or risk) in the portfolio declines. The object of diversifying a portfolio, then, is to achieve a condition where the portfolio can be expected to provide a return reasonably in line with the return expected of an individual position. It's not unlike flipping a coin: flip once and there's as much chance to lose as to win; flip 20 times and the outcome is likely to be close to the 50-50 you expected.

Diversification comes at a price, however. The more positions you add, the more work is expended in finding the positions and the harder it is to keep abreast of developments that affect them. In addition, commission and transaction costs rise as positions become smaller. The question then is to determine the degree of diversification that is optimal.

INVESTING WITH THE ODDS IN YOUR FAVOR

If we are able to select positions that offered no better than 50-50 odds, all we could hope for over time is to break even. Unless we can count on being consistently lucky, we need to tip the odds in our favor. That is, for example, risk $1 to make $1 where the odds favor that we'll win twice and lose once in three chances.

Virtually all option pricing theory is based on log-normal stock price distribution. While the log-normal curve is not 100% accurate (the actual curve is slightly steeper at the center, slightly thinner at the sides, and trails off into fatter "tails" on both ends), it's probably fair to say that stock price movement conforms to the log-normal pattern about two-thirds of the time. Thus, by pricing options on the basis of the log-normal curve as we have in this book, the odds become about 2-to-1 in favor of a position working out as expected.

The Two Components of "Odds"

What is not generally appreciated is that the "odds" have two components:

1. The Win Ratio

2. The Payoff Ratio

For example, in a four-horse race, assuming all horses were equal, we'd expect to win once in four races, on average, a win ratio of 25%. For even "odds," the payoff ratio should be 4-to-1: bet $1 to make $4. That gives us a 25% chance of winning $4 (i.e., 25% × $4/$1) making the odds 1-to-1.

Change either the win ratio or the payoff ratio and the odds no longer remain even. If our horse has an expected 50% win ratio, the odds become 2-to-1 (50% × $4/$1). Or, we'd have the same 2-to-1 odds if the win ratio remained 25% but the payoff ratio changed to 8-to-1 (25% × $8/$1).

Why this is important in investing will now become evident. Suppose you had to choose between these two investments:

	Win Ratio	Payoff Ratio	Odds
#1	90%	$2-to-$1	1.8-to-1
#2	20%	$9-to-$1	1.8-to-1

Notice that although the odds are the same for both, the risk is substantially different. In the first, the chance of being wiped out is 10%. In the second, the chance of being wiped out is 80%. Clearly, your investment planning must be tied not to the "odds" or the payoff ratio but to the expected win ratio.

MANAGING RISK

With that in mind, let's now add a second objective to managing a portfolio:

Objective #1. Achieve a condition where the portfolio can be expected to provide a return reasonably in line with the return expected of an individual position.

Objective # 2. Reduce the risk of being wiped out (or of losing money) to an acceptable level.

HOW DIVERSIFICATION REDUCES RISK OF LOSS

Whether a portfolio contains one position or many similar positions, the odds of "winning" an expected return remain unchanged. Paradoxically, however, the greater the number of positions, the smaller the odds become of "losing." Consider, again, the situation where the odds in your favor are 66.7%, or 2-to-1. In this case, the win ratio is 66 1/3% (i.e., you win 2-of-3 times) and the payoff ratio is $3-to-$1. If you invest your entire stake in one position, your risk of being wiped out is 1-in-3. Split your capital between two *unrelated* positions whose outcomes are not interdependent, however, and the risk of losing your entire stake shrinks from 1-in-3 to 1-in-9, as follows:

Position #1:

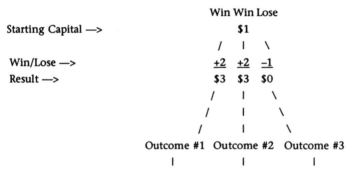

```
                          Win Win Lose
Starting Capital —>            $1
                             /  |  \
Win/Lose —>                  +2 +2 -1
Result —>                    $3 $3 $0
                            /   |   \
                           /    |    \
                          /     |     \
                  Outcome #1  Outcome #2  Outcome #3
                       |         |         |
```

Position #2

	Win	Win	Lose		Win	Win	Lose		Win	Win	Lose
Starting Capital —>		$1				$1				$1	
	/	|	\		/	|	\		/	|	\
Win/Lose—>	+2	+2	-1		+2	+2	-1		+2	+2	-1
Result —>	$3	$3	$0		$3	$3	$0		$3	$3	$0
+ Position #1—>	3	3	3		3	3	3		0	0	0
Capital —>	$6	$6	$3		$6	$6	$3		$3	$3	$0

The example above has nine possible outcomes. Notice that "$0," the risk of being wiped out, has dropped from 1-in-3 to 1-in-9. The odds, however, haven't changed, they remain 2-to-1. (The sum won in the 9 possible returns is $36, or an average of $4 on each $2 investment.) If we increased the number of unrelated positions to 10, the odds of being wiped out would fall to just 1-in-59,000.

> (*Note*: All investment positions whose values are derived from an underlying common stock are dependent to a degree on the movement of the market. Adding positions does not eliminate the risk that a sharp adverse market move will cause all stocks—and options on those stocks—to move against you. But only about 30% of a stock's movement typically results from the movement of the market. The balance, 70%, is related to events that are perceived to affect the fortunes of that one company or companies in related activities. By diversifying, the object is to reach a position where such events in one issue are likely to be offset by events of an opposite nature in another so that the portfolio provides the indicated return.)

As previously illustrated, the risk of being wiped out depends not on the overall odds but on the win ratio. one option may have a win ratio of 1-to-1, another 1-in-10, yet both may offer 2-to-1 odds. Exhibit 15.1 shows how the probability of wipeout and, consequently, the need for diversification, increases as the win ratio declines. The number of option positions in the portfolio are shown on the left, the figures at the far right of each line (in **bold**) indicate the probability that all positions will "lose." (Thus, with a win ratio of 2-to-1, if there is only one position in the portfolio, the probability of that one position "losing" and the total investment being wiped out is 33%; with two positions, the probability drops to 11%, with three it falls to 4%, etc.)

Exhibit 15.1 Example A: Probability of Unsuccessful Positions

Portfolio #1 — "Win" Ratio: 2-to-1

No. of Psns	0	1	2	3	4	5	6	7	8	9	10	11	12
1	0.67	**0.33**											
2	0.44	0.44	**0.11**										
3	0.30	0.44	0.22	**0.04**									
4	0.20	0.40	0.30	0.10	**0.01**								
5	0.13	0.33	0.33	0.16	0.04	**0.00**							
6	0.09	0.26	0.33	0.22	0.08	0.02	**0.00**						
7	0.06	0.20	0.31	0.26	0.13	0.04	0.01	**0.00**					
8	0.04	0.16	0.27	0.27	0.17	0.07	0.02	0.00	**0.00**				
9	0.03	0.12	0.23	0.27	0.20	0.10	0.03	0.01	0.00	**0.00**			
10	0.02	0.09	0.20	0.26	0.23	0.14	0.06	0.02	0.00	0.00	**0.00**		
11	0.01	0.06	0.16	0.24	0.24	0.17	0.08	0.03	0.01	0.00	0.00	**0.00**	
12	0.01	0.05	0.13	0.21	0.24	0.19	0.11	0.05	0.01	0.00	0.00	0.00	**0.00**

Portfolio #2 — "Win" Ratio: 1-to-1

No. of Psns	0	1	2	3	4	5	6	7	8	9	10	11	12
1	0.50	**0.50**											
2	0.25	0.50	**0.25**										
3	0.13	0.38	0.38	**0.13**									
4	0.06	0.25	0.38	0.25	**0.06**								
5	0.03	0.16	0.31	0.31	0.16	**0.03**							
6	0.02	0.09	0.23	0.31	0.23	0.09	**0.02**						
7	0.01	0.05	0.16	0.27	0.27	0.16	0.05	**0.01**					
8	0.00	0.03	0.11	0.22	0.27	0.22	0.11	0.03	**0.00**				
9	0.00	0.02	0.07	0.16	0.25	0.25	0.16	0.07	0.02	**0.00**			
10	0.00	0.01	0.04	0.12	0.21	0.25	0.21	0.12	0.04	0.01	**0.00**		
11	0.00	0.01	0.03	0.08	0.16	0.23	0.23	0.16	0.08	0.03	0.01	**0.00**	
12	0.00	0.00	0.02	0.05	0.12	0.19	0.23	0.19	0.12	0.05	0.02	0.00	**0.00**

Exhibit 15.1 Continued

		0	1	2	3	4	5	6	7	8	9	10	11	12
	1	0.33	**0.67**						Portfolio #3					
/	2	0.11	0.44	**0.44**					"Win" Ratio: 1-to-2					
I	3	0.04	0.22	0.44	**0.30**									
I	4	0.01	0.10	0.30	-0.40	**0.20**								
I	5	0.00	0.04	0.16	0.33	0.33	**0.13**							
I	6	0.00	0.02	0.08	0.22	0.33	0.26	**0.09**						
	7	0.00	0.01	0.04	0.13	0.26	0.31	0.20	**0.06**					
No.	8	0.00	0.00	0.02	0.07	0.17	0.27	0.27	0.16	**0.04**				
	9	0.00	0.00	0.01	0.03	0.10	0.20	0.27	0.23	0.12	**0.03**			
of	10	0.00	0.00	0.00	0.02	0.06	0.14	0.23	0.26	0.20	0.09	**0.02**		
	11	0.00	0.00	0.00	0.01	0.03	0.08	0.17	0.24	0.24	0.16	0.06	**0.01**	
Psns	12	0.00	0.00	0.00	0.00	0.01	0.05	0.11	0.19	0.24	0.21	0.13	0.05	**0.01**
	1	0.10	**0.90**						Portfolio #4					
/	2	0.01	0.18	**0.81**					"Win" Ratio: 1-to-10					
I	3	0.00	0.03	0.24	**0.73**									
I	4	0.00	0.00	0.05	0.29	**0.66**								
I	5	0.00	0.00	0.01	0.07	0.33	**0.59**							
I	6	0.00	0.00	0.00	0.01	0.10	0.35	**0.53**						
	7	0.00	0.00	0.00	0.00	0.02	0.12	0.37	**0.48**					
No.	8	0.00	0.00	0.00	0.00	0.00	0.03	0.15	0.38	**0.43**				
	9	0.00	0.00	0.00	0.00	0.00	0.01	0.04	0.17	0.39	**0.39**			
of	10	0.00	0.00	0.00	0.00	0.00	0.00	0.01	0.06	0.19	0.39	**0.35**		
	11	0.00	0.00	0.00	0.00	0.00	0.00	0.00	0.02	0.07	0.21	0.38	**0.31**	
Psns	12	0.00	0.00	0.00	0.00	0.00	0.00	0.00	0.00	0.02	0.09	0.23	0.38	**0.28**

HOW DIVERSIFICATION INCREASES THE PROBABILITY OF PROFIT

Exhibit 15.1 shows the probability of a portfolio being wiped out, but it doesn't make obvious how often the portfolio is likely to produce a profit. To determine that, we must consider both the win ratio and the payoff ratio.

Here are another two portfolios containing positions with odds of 1.8-to-1, but with different win and payoff ratios.

Portfolio	Win Ratio	Payoff Ratio	Odds
# 1	9-to-1 (90%)	2-to-1	1.8-to-1
# 2	6-to-4 (60%)	3-to-1	1.8-to-1

Figures in **bold** in Exhibit 15.2 show the probabilities that the portfolio will turn a profit, figures in *italics* the likelihood of breakeven, and figures in light type show the probability of loss. Notice that if the odds are the same, the portfolio with the higher win ratio and lower payoff ratio offers the greater probability of turning a profit.

Exhibit 15.2 Example B: Probability of Unsuccessful Positions

---

		Number of Unsuccessful Positions									
		0	1	2	3	4	5	6	7	8	9
	1	**0.90**	0.10								
/	2	**0.81**	0.18	0.01							
l	3	**0.73**	**0.24**	*0.03*	0.00						
l	4	**0.66**	**0.29**	*0.05*	0.00	0.00					
l	5	**0.59**	**0.33**	**0.07**	0.01	0.00	0.00				
l	6	**0.53**	**0.35**	**0.10**	*0.01*	0.00	0.00	0.00			
	7	**0.48**	**0.37**	**0.12**	**0.02**	0.00	0.00	0.00	0.00		
No.	8	**0.43**	**0.38**	**0.15**	**0.03**	0.00	0.00	0.00	0.00	0.00	
	9	**0.39**	**0.39**	**0.17**	**0.04**	0.01	0.00	0.00	0.00	0.00	0.00
of	10	**0.35**	**0.39**	**0.19**	**0.06**	0.01	0.00	0.00	0.00	0.00	0.00
	11	**0.31**	**0.38**	**0.21**	**0.07**	0.02	**0.00**	0.00	0.00	0.00	0.00
Psns	12	**0.28**	**0.38**	**0.23**	**0.09**	0.02	**0.00**	0.00	0.00	0.00	0.00

Portfolio #1
"Win" Ratio: 90%
"Payoff" Ratio: 2-to-1

Exhibit 15.2 Continued

		Number of Unsuccessful Positions											
		0	1	2	3	4	5	6	7	8	9		
	1	0.60	0.40										
/	2	0.36	0.48	0.16									
I	3	0.22	0.43	0.29	0.06								
I	4	0.13	0.35	0.35	0.15	0.03							
I	5	0.08	0.26	0.35	0.23	0.08	0.01						
I	6	0.05	0.19	0.31	0.28	0.14	0.04	0.00					
	7	0.03	0.13	0.26	0.29	0.19	0.08	0.02	0.00				
No.	8	0.02	0.09	0.21	0.28	0.23	0.12	0.04	0.01	0.00			
	9	0.01	0.06	0.16	0.25	0.25	0.17	0.07	0.02	0.00	0.00		
of	10	0.01	0.04	0.12	0.21	0.25	0.20	0.11	0.04	0.01	0.00	0.00	
	11	0.00	0.03	0.09	0.18	0.24	0.22	0.15	0.07	0.02	0.01	0.00	0.00
Psns	12	0.00	0.02	0.06	0.14	0.21	0.23	0.18	0.10	0.04	0.01	0.00	0.00	0.00

Portfolio #2
"Win" Ratio: 60%
"Payoff" Ratio: 3-to-1

Note: A Lotus-based spreadsheet (complete with cell formulas) for creating these probability tables appears at the end of this chapter in Appendix 15.A.

HOW MUCH DIVERSIFICATION DO YOU NEED?

Whether we are betting or investing, we must keep in sight the difference between probability and possibility. It is improbable, for example, to flip 50 heads in a row but not impossible. Similarly, if we could depend on aberrant positions to "misbehave" to an equal degree so that an unexpected rise in one offsets an unexpected decline in another, the optimum degree of diversification could be reasonably pinpointed. Most investment advisers recommend that a portfolio of 10 to 15 positions is sufficient to eliminate company-related risk in a stock portfolio. Clearly, however, the degree of diversification must depend on the win ratio of the issues in the portfolio, which means that far more diversification is required in a portfolio of naked options than in a portfolio of stocks.

On the other hand, there is the downside to diversification mentioned earlier. In all, then, basing diversification on the risk (relative volatility) of the issues in the portfolio, the following general guide suggests itself:

Type of Issue	Relative Volatility	Number of Issues
Covered Calls	55%	8-to-10
Common Stocks	100%	10-to-15
Short Options	350%	15-to-20
Long Options	1,000%	20-to-40*

Note: For higher risk options, further diversification is wise. In a hedged naked option portfolio, as described in Chapter 13, this total may be split between the two sides of the portfolio. If offsetting positions on the two sides of the hedge are in the same industry, somewhat less diversification may be acceptable.

HOW TO DIVERSIFY

For proper diversification, there are four requirements:

1. Individual positions should be in different industries which, as far as possible, are not interdependent.

2. The size of each position should be reasonably comparable.

3. The relative volatility of positions should be within a reasonable range. (Relative volatilities should be based on the expected value of the option at expiration and not on the price at which the option is trading.)

4. Expiration dates should be somewhat staggered.

Each "infraction" of these requirements reduces the diversification. For example, in a portfolio of 10 issues, each issue normally pulls one-tenth of the weight. So if one issue drops 10%, the portfolio falls 1%. If that one issue were twice the size of the others, however, the drop in the portfolio would be about twice as steep. Similarly, if the relative volatility of one issue doubles, it, too, would pull twice the weight.

WHEN TO CLOSE OUT POSITIONS

1. Positions are normally closed out when there is a substantial change in the outlook for the underlying security.

2. In addition, options may be closed out if they have swung from being drastically undervalued to drastically overvalued, or vice versa, but only if it would be profitable to do so after commissions.

3. Over time, as positions grow in size in comparison to the average issue in the portfolio, it will be necessary to cut them back. As a rule of thumb, a posi-

tion that is three times the size of the average position can be assumed to be overbalancing others in
the portfolio. Smaller positions, however, may be
viewed as pieces of one position.

4. Relative volatilities also change; positions whose
relative volatilities have fallen well below or risen
well above the range targeted should be realigned
for the former will pull too little weight while the
latter will over dominate.

5. In the case of a hedged portfolio, each side should
be diversified. If possible, it is desirable to hold options on companies in the same industries on each
side of the hedge. Further information for diversifying a hedged portfolio will be found in Chapters 12
and 14.

6. Further information for rolling out of covered call
positions will be found in Chapter 11.

Once again, rebalancing a portfolio should be done
with an eye on commissions and expiration dates.

APPENDIX 15.A
Lotus Probability Spreadsheet

Row/Col	A	B	C	D	E	F	G	H	I	J	K	L	M	N
1								Win Ratio: 0.6						
2						Number of Unsuccessful Positions								
3			0	1	2	3	4	5	6	7	8	9	10	11
4														
5						PROBABILITIES								
6		1	0.60	0.40										
7	/	2	0.36	0.48	0.16									
8	I	3	0.22	0.43	0.29	0.06								
9	I	4	0.13	0.35	0.35	0.15	0.03							
10	I	5	0.08	0.26	0.35	0.23	0.08	0.01						
11	I	6	0.05	0.19	0.31	0.28	0.14	0.04	0.00					
12		7	0.03	0.13	0.26	0.29	0.19	0.08	0.02	0.00				
13	No.	8	0.02	0.09	0.21	0.28	0.23	0.12	0.04	0.01	0.00			
14		9	0.01	0.06	0.16	0.25	0.25	0.17	0.07	0.02	0.00	0.00		
15	of	10	0.01	0.04	0.12	0.21	0.25	0.20	0.11	0.04	0.01	0.00	0.00	
16		11	0.00	0.03	0.09	0.18	0.24	0.22	0.15	0.07	0.02	0.01	0.00	0.00
17	Psns	12	0.00	0.02	0.06	0.14	0.21	0.23	0.18	0.10	0.04	0.01	0.00	0.00

Note: If the ratio of "winning" positions is less than 0.5, instead of the **"Win"** Ratio, enter the **"Loss"** Ratio. Then, instead of "Number of **Unsuccessful** Positions," the table will show the "Number of **Successful** Positions."

Cell Formulas for Lotus Spreadsheet for Probability of Win/Loss Ratios

J1	Insert the ratio of winning positions to losing positions
C3..?3	Data fill beginning with "0" adding "1" each step across to whatever Column desired
B6..Bn	Data fill beginning with "1" adding "1" down to whatever row desired
C6	+$J$1^B6; copy down to bottom row
D6	(1-$J$1)^$B6
D7..?n	@IF(C6" "#AND#D6" ",,C6*(1-$J$1)+D6*$J$1,,@IF(C6" "#AND#D6=" " ",,(1-$J$1)^$B7,," ")); copy down to bottom row and across to last column

Setting Realistic
Expectations and a
Look to the Future

And now, in summing up, we discuss how to measure investment performance against realistic benchmarks so that we need no longer feel like an inept fool when friends play the game: "My stock tripled in three weeks."

THE JOHN DALY SYNDROME

What captures the public's imagination are the big hitters. John Daly leaped to stardom in 1991 when, as a last minute replacement—after 15 others proved unavailable—he entered and won the coveted PGA golf tournament.

The understudy who comes on stage at the last minute and rises to stardom is the stuff fairy tales are made of. Immediately dubbed the "new hit" on tour, fans lined up five deep to see Daly whenever he appeared. But what drew them wasn't Daly's successes; during the next dozen months, Daly failed to qualify (and was dropped from the tournament) in eight events, withdrew once, and managed to finish in the top ten (of the original 72 entrants) only three times. Still the crowds queued up. While other players—Freddy Couples and Davis Love III—were winning the tournaments, Daly was hitting the humongous drives. Daly could hit a golf ball longer than any pro on tour, though, unfortunately, not always straight down the fairway.

The same fascination holds in the investment world. What investors line up to hear about is not a boring story of relentlessly compounded results but the season's "winningest" fund manager, the guy who hit the humongous drives. I never heard a friend brag that his portfolio was up $X\%$ for the year but I've heard many crow about XYZ bought a week ago that's already up three points, or XYX that more than doubled since they bought it. I can't help feeling envious as hell when I hear those stories, though sometimes it occurs to me that I should have asked whether they did as well across the board or were there other stocks they held that collapsed as those rose.

It's fun to tell your friends about your big wins. Indeed, who's to say that you can't parlay one big win into many and amass a sizable poke? But when you go for the big hit, those mis-hits seem to get in the way, annoyingly wiping out your gains.

I said a number of times in this book that few investors can call the market successfully: I have models, in fact, that call the market with amazing accuracy. Contrary to what might be expected, however, it's hard to use them to make money, for the models don't predict when the swings will occur. A market turn may come a few days after an upturn is forecast, a few weeks later, or even a year or more later. In the interim, the market waffles, a scenario described by those who have researched market price movement from the perspective of the relatively new science "Chaos." While it waffles, even if you have the stomach for it, carrying costs mount and returns shade off.

Of course, in few areas is "timing" a price movement as important as in naked option trading. Unless you can accurately forecast both the direction of the price movement and the timeframe, you're likely to find that hedged strategies pay off with better results (and fewer ulcers). As a covered call writer, for example, whether the market waffles or moves as you hoped, returns are usually handsome relative to the risk. For those willing to take on greater risk, hedging short calls against long calls also offers a better opportunity to earn consistent (and generous) returns.

SETTING REALISTIC EXPECTATIONS

One of the hardships of choosing conservative strategies is that you're at a disadvantage in swapping "My XZX doubled in three months!" stories with cronies. After all, it doesn't count for much to report that your ZXZ jumped 25% but that calls you wrote against it absorbed much of the gain. If you are able to listen to their success stories with a smile that you don't find necessary to force without adding, "As the Bible sayeth, how does it benefit a man if he gains one success but his portfolio does not prosper?", you're probably suited for strategies that are more likely to pay off consistently with superior returns over time.

Yet, be prepared that even a hedged strategy doesn't insure a steady advance in the value of a portfolio. There will be setbacks—sharp ones in a long call/short call hedge—more moderate ones in a covered call portfolio. Even "rolling" won't always help. Comparing performance with the market should be avoided, too, particularly in years when the market takes a particularly brisk move, for a hedged portfolio marches to its own drummer. Ultimately, however, though your portfolio is constructed of—and relies for its performance on—individual issues, the measure of its performance are the results overall, not of any individual issue or two.

CHALLENGE FOR THE FUTURE

The strategies described in this book are based on statistical probability, a discipline that attempts to fit a smooth curve over sets of data. Statistics has severe shortcomings, however, in part because data that does not fit beneath a curve may offer greater insights into market movement than data that does, in part because in attempting to devise tests to tame errant data, statisticians may, inadvertently, simply design tests that prove what they determined to prove.

An example of this is back-testing. Using multiple regressions, statisticians attempt to find data series that would forecast observed phenomena. By playing back interest rates, free market reserves, consumer debt, and other economic series against the market, for example, statisticians look for combinations that would have forecast past ups and downs in the market. But their results must be viewed with some skepticism for they are achieved with the benefit of hindsight. Had the hoped-for results not been forthcoming, they would have merely broadened the search until amenable data series were found. If interest rates proved useless, changes in interest rates would be tested. Ultimately, even rainfall patterns might come under their microscope, anything whose relationship to the market might be rationalized, if it produced the desired results. Thus, we might well find that most past events, however random, could have been forecast during a specific period with the aid of some series of data or other.

Whether it would work in the future, however, is another story. Some statisticians argue that they can avoid this "trap" by regressing data from one past period (e.g., 1900–1970) and testing it in a later period (e.g., 1971–1990). But this reasoning is equally specious, for had the desired results not been observed during the test period (1971–1990), the data series regressed in the earlier period (1900–1970) would be altered until they were.

In any event, it seems unlikely that new systems for successfully forecasting absolute or relative stock price movement will come out of statistical disciplines for they have been exhaustively researched and tested. Literally hundreds of investment houses have spent thousands of hours—perhaps tens of thousands of hours—multiple regressing economic and market data that might conceivably correlate with market movement, and applying the entire gamut of statistical tests in an attempt to gain a trading edge. What can be found in one shop, inevitably, can and is found in others, for with high-speed computers, this is a trivial exercise. The result, of course, is that if a real advantage is discovered in one shop, it is also discovered in others, and whatever advantage may have existed is quickly dissipated as competing shops attempt to capitalize on the same slim advantage.

Worse yet, often such "advantages" are ephemeral or periodic, existing in the past but not continuing or persisting in the present or future. For there is a real danger in assuming that correlations that existed in the past are actually cause and effect . . . that multiple regressions of past data that show a correlation satisfactory to a statistician are more than quirks. There is an interesting paradox here. It is usually necessary to base future predictions on the confluence of data that in the past has suggested, from a statistical perspective, the likelihood of specific events occurring in the future. Yet it is dangerous to place great reliance on the likelihood that the events tested did, indeed, have a cause and effect relationship. For statisticians are, in some respects, guilty of circular reasoning. Here, they say, our regressions show that there is a correlation between events j, k, and l, and the likelihood of X occurring. What they often fail to appreciate is that they set out to discover what data streams could predict, according to their discipline, the occurrence of X, and when they find data that appears to predict X, they report that they can predict X based on j, k, and l. What they fail to report, however, is that their search continued over ever wider fields until they achieved the "fit" they wished. Indeed, had they found that traffic light patterns in lower Manhattan during the past 10 years or, as some researchers have actually suggested, the length of women's hemlines, correlates with the health of the economy, they could have rationalized, after the fact, that it is logical for such data to be predictive of X.

The fact that major investment consultants such as the Frank Russell organization now treat back-testing with a large degree of skepticism doesn't seem to phase the true believers. Russell, as well as other companies in this field, are inundated by would-be investment managers who offer up as proof of their ability to beat the market back tests of sophisticated systems they devised. Indeed, James Gleick, in his book "Chaos," describing the activities of one of the great names in this field, noted that "Lorenz realized . . . hiding within a particular system could be more than one stable solution. An observer might see one kind of behavior over a very long time, yet a completely different kind of behavior could be just as natural for the system." The increasing unreliability of the Value Line ranking system over time may be just such a case.

Needless to say, one normally has greatest confidence in systems that have worked in practice over a period of time rather than in back-testing, though it is difficult to escape the nagging doubt that even then, the results came about entirely as a matter of chance. While there is a momentum factor that suggests that if a fund is doing well relative to the market it is likely to continue to do well, not infrequently, the funds that performed best in a past period turn out to be the worst performers in subsequent periods. In a universe of funds as large as now exists, some number of funds will do better than others during any one year simply on the basis of probability. And of those funds that are on top one year, simply as a matter of probability, some portion will be on top in year two, and some portion of those will be on top in year three, etc. Indeed, we have all heard of the scam about the horse racing buff who ignored a tip on Whirl Away from a tout who claimed to have devised a system. Still skeptical even after Whirl Away won, the horse player ignored the tout the next day too, but again his selection won. At last, convinced, the player plunked down a wad of dough on the tout's selection for day three. What he never knew was that he was one of an original group of 64 horse players the tout approached on day one. Eight were given the name of one horse, another group of eight the name of a second, a third group of eight got the name of a third, etc. Of course, eight players of the original 64 received the name of the winning horse on day one. On day 2, the tout returned to those eight "winners" and gave each the name of a different horse running on day 2. In that way, he was sure that 1 of the original 64 horse players would have been touted onto two successive winners.

USING VALUE LINE'S RANKING SYSTEMS TO BETTER ADVANTAGE

If multiple regressions of past data and other conventional statistical tests aren't likely to provide investors with a better method of selecting stocks, is there any hope of beating the market? I believe there is. One way would be to alter Value Line's common stock ranking system to correct some of its shortcomings. Notice, for example, that both the *Value Line Options* and Value Line convertible ranking systems have had substantially better results than Value Line's common stock ranking system. There are significant reasons why:

1. Rather than trying to cover a broad range of stocks for which they may not be suited, each is directed to a specific subset of securities.

2. Performance is scored as it is in the real investment world, after transaction costs and with income included, not simply in terms of appreciation.

3. Risk is taken into consideration: performance is not measured absolutely, but in relation to risk.

Don't Try to Be All Things for All Securities

Value Line set out to develop a common stock ranking system that would predict relative stock price movement for all stocks. The system that evolved proved predictive of growth stock price movement but not of the relative performance of cyclicals, natural resource stocks, or large dividend paying stocks. Had it acknowledged that the system worked well for growth stocks and directed its focus there, it might have not only posted a better job in discriminating between growth stocks, but it also may have devised effective systems for other types of stocks.

Account for Income

It is plain silly for an investment system to measure its performance by yardsticks other than those used by the investors expected to use it. By ignoring dividends and transaction costs, Value Line not only renders the performance results of the common stock ranking system meaningless, but inadvertently frustrates its efforts to develop the best possible system. Part of the reason that the Value Line convertible and option ranking systems have performed so much better than the common stock ranking system is evident in their literature. Where applicable, they add dividend yield to and subtract transaction costs from the expected relative price performance of each issue and then re-rank all issues on the basis of expected total return. This is particularly germane when the concept of risk is considered, for it becomes clear that higher risk is not always the avenue toward higher returns.

Risk

Investment returns must, of course, be related to risk. While Value Line advises subscribers to choose higher-risk stocks for higher returns in a rising market (or poorer returns in a falling market), no allowance for risk is included in the common stock ranks. The options and convertible ranking systems, in contrast, rank issues on the basis of expected total return *relative to the risk in the issue*. It is likely that performance of a common stock ranking system would be enhanced similarly.

Other Systems

Needless to say, growth is just one criteria for selecting stocks. Other criteria—price to book value, price to earnings, small-cap over-the-counter stocks versus large-cap stocks—come into prominence during one period or another only to fall back in favor of others. No system, no matter how selective, will work all the time. One of the most promising approaches, according to its developers, is a system that combines several discrete systems under the umbrella of a "system director." In the same way that the Value Line ranking system ranks the expected performance of individual stocks, this system ranks the expected performance of the different investment systems so as to steer investments into areas deemed likely to lead the market at the appropriate time.

The relatively new science "chaos" has not proven to be much help in predicting market swings as yet but it may prove capable of detecting the rotation in these investment patterns. Inevitably, however, the market appears to be not unlike a simple machine whose movement is determined in part by inertia and in part by mob psychology, so it would not be surprising if, when a breakthrough is achieved, it was made by a team which combined psychologists, physicists and mathematicians.

May you grow old slowly and prosperous rapidly.

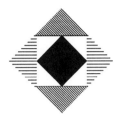

Index

Compaq Computers, 34, 35
Composite Index, *see* Value Line
Consumer debt, 248
Contingent orders, 14, 15, 19
Conversion, 53, 59
  value, 56, 60
Convertible(s), 49, 53, 54, 56, 60
  see Plain, Preferred, Zero-coupon
  bond, 63-69
  preferred stock, 51, 52, 55
  ranking system, *see* Value Line
Cost basis, 184, 185
Covenants, 56
Covered call, 20, 49-62, 148, 187
  debasing, 59-61
  funds, 188
  portfolio writing, 31
  position, 139, 172, 180, 184, 188
  reason, 53-55
  recommendations, 188
  writer, 9, 61, 247
  writing, 30, 31, 59, 143, 169-191,
    193-197, 199
  definition, 171-173
Covered option, *see* Naked option
Covered portfolio writing, 30, 193-
    197, 199
  entry, 194-196
Covered writer, 135, 138-139, 172,
    174, 176
  investment, 139
  risk, 173
Covered writing, 150, 173
  position, 138
Cox-Ross-Rubenstein model, 133
Cyclical stock, 197, 253

D

Daly, John, *see* John
Day orders, 19
Deep-in-the-money calls, 176, 177
Derivatives, 49, 51
Diagonal spread, 72
Disclosure, 171
Discount

broker, 15, 77, 203
rate, 106
Distribution, 118
  see Log-normal, Normal, Probability
  curve, 117, 118
Diversification, 188, 206, 210, 211,
    212, 214, 223, 229-243
  amount, 239-240
  curve, *see* Log-normal
  process, 208-209, 240-241
  profit probability, 237-239
  reasons, 229-230
  requirements, 240-241
  risk of loss reduction, 233-237
Diversified
  portfolio, 208, 211
  position, 212
Dividend(s), 3, 27, 30, 36, 53, 55,
    87, 94, 98-99, 105, 178, 185,
    253
  income, 45
  payout ratio, 89
  yield, 100, 253-254
Dividends-to-earnings payout ratio,
    89
Dollar value, 14, 194, 207
Dow Jones
  Average, 34
  Industrial Average (DJIA), 29
Downside protection, 176, 180, 187,
    194, 195

E

Earnings
  see Dividends-to-earnings,
    Price/earnings
  forecasts, 89
  growth, 89
  rate, 87, 89, 93
  surprises, 91
Eisenstadt, Sam, 197
Equity/equities, 43
  funds, see Value Line
  options, 10, 12, 39
  portfolio managers, 197

259

Index

Probability, 8, 109-111, 112-118,
120, 141, 150, 235, 238, 239
see Statistical, Weighted
distribution, 130-132
Profit(s), 6, 13, 45, 50, 55, 71, 74-77,
79, 87, 93, 136, 137, 170, 173,
174, 180, 181, 187, 202, 204,
205, 210, 238
see Before-commission, Guaranteed
forecasts, 91
forecasting, 96-99
opportunities, 16, 37
potential, 180, 181
see Annualized
probability, *see* Diversification
protection, 181
reports, 91
Profit/loss profiles, 53, 54, 72, 112
Prospectus, 56, 57, 62, 64
Protection, *see* Downside, Loss, Profit
Put(s), 2, 25-31, 45
see At-the-money, Buy, Calls, Sell,
Short
buying, 143
insurance, 27
options, 3
premium, 31, 206
value, 159
writing, 143

R

Rate of return, 139
Ratio spread, 72
Realistic expectations, 245-255
setting, 247-248
Reinvested capital, 111
Relative prices, 88
Relative volatility, 41, 69, 112, 126-
127, 137, 173, 189-190, 207,
208, 212-214, 241, 242
see Implied
Retail brokerage network, 64
Return, 80, 137, 140, 173, 174, 177,
220, 223, 235, 254

see Annual, Annualized, Guaranteed, Investment, Rate
Return on capital, 109-132, 134, 135
Return on invested capital, 111
Return on investment (ROI), 68,
109, 111, 138, 160, 202, 203,
212
Return to expiration, 184
Revenue opportunities, 12
Reward characteristics, 187
Reward/risk
basis, 105
ratio, 31, 80, 109, 111-112, 128-
130, 173-175, 177, 178, 213
Risk, 9, 44, 57, 69, 81, 93, 112, 126-
127, 130, 135-137, 138-140,
171, 176, 177, 189, 188, 193,
194, 199, 204, 209-213, 219,
229-243, 254
see Added, Buyer, Common stock,
Company-related, Covered
writer, Loss, Negative, Option, Reward/risk, Risk-free,
Seller
addition, 196
characteristics, 187
determination, negative risk comparison, 141-159
management, 233
measurement, 141-160
options, 240
Risk of loss, *see* Diversification
Risk-adjusted spread, 202
Risk-free interest rate, 7, 35, 36
Rolling, 180-182, 184, 242, 248
choice, 185-187
Russel, Frank, 250, 251

S

Savage, Bob, 170
Scholes, Myron, 26, 34
see Black-Scholes
Securities and Exchange Commission (SEC), 62
accounting rules, 170

Index

Upside potential, 194

V

Valuation measures, 98
Value, 7, 54
  see Call, Conversion, Expected, Ex-
    piration, Intrinsic, Invest-
    ment, Market, Present, Put,
    Tangible, Time, Zero-coupon
Value Line, 39
  see Index
  common stock ranking system, 91,
    95, 252, 253
    usage, 93-94
  Composite Index, 13
  convertible ranking system, 103,
    104, 252, 253
  equity funds, 196
  Investment Survey, 86
  option ranking system, 103-104,
    253
  Options, 40, 174, 188, 205, 252
    ability, 215
    usage, 189-191
  performance results, 94-95, 100,
    105
  ranking system(s), 85-106, 196, 205
    usage, 252-255
  stock selection system, 85
Value at expiration, 137, 137, 140
Value ratios, *see* Price-to-book
Vertical spread, 72
Volatility, 7, 8, 31, 119, 126-127,
    136, 140, 142, 148, 189, 196,
    220
  see Future, Historic, Implied, Price,
    Relative

W

Wall Street Journal, 2, 28
Warrants, 49
Wealth, spreading, 71-82
Weighted probability, 147
Williams, J.B., 87, 89

Win ratio, 232-235, 238
Win/loss ratios, 247-248
Win-win strategy, 45
Wipeout, 235
Writer, 2, 9
  see Call, Covered, Naked, Option
Writing, *see* Call, Covered, Put

Y

Yield, *see* Dividend

Z

Zero-coupon convertible(s), 61, 64-67
  bond, 68
  value, 66

FOR HELP IN MANAGING YOUR MONEY . . .

ALL OPTION PROGRAMS
in this book
ON COMPUTER DISK

The option programs laid out in Chapters 9, 10, 11, 13, and 15 can be purchased on disk (with full documentation) ready to install in your computer for immediate use in managing your options portfolio. (Programs on this disk have been upgraded with enhancements that could not be incorporated in the basic programs in the book without substantially increasing the book's length.) The disk INCLUDES EACH OF THE FOLLOWING PROGRAMS:

To Evaluate Options using *Traditional Methods* (see Chapter 10):

CALL BUYING   CALL SELLING
PUT BUYING   PUT SELLING
COVERED WRITING

To Evaluate Options based on *"Negative Risk"* (see Chapter 10, 11, and 13):

CALL BUYING   CALL SELLING
PUT BUYING   PUT SELLING
COVERED WRITING

Plus . . . Evaluating Probability (Chapter 15):

THE PROBABILITY OF A POSITION BEING SUCCESSFUL OR UNSUCCESSFUL

---------------------- TO ORDER ----------------------
To: Allan S. Lyons
      Post Office Box 474
      Pinehurst, NC 28374

Price: $99

Yes, please send me a computer disk with all of these programs ready for use in managing my options portfolio plus full documentation. I understand that I must have LOTUS©, or Lotus-compatible software such as SYMPHONY™ to use these programs. Order must be accompanied by check or money order for $99. Please allow up to four weeks for delivery.

Name: _____

Address: _____ Zip: _____

Specify: 3 1/2" Disk:_____   5 1/4" Disk: _____